The Magic of the COTSWOLD WAY

By the same author

A Kind of Magic
Another Kind of Magic
The Green Years
The Archers Country Cookbook
Country Cooking from Pebble Mill
From Acre End
A Drop O' Wine
Cotswold Privies
The Cotswold Country Cookbook
Where the Windrush Flows
Wychwood: The Secret Cotswold Forest
The Stripling Thames
Privies Galore
Country Wines: To Make, Drink and Cook with
Village Christmases

THE MAGIC OF THE COTSWOLD WAY

Mollie Harris

Leave only footprints
Take only memories

ALAN SUTTON PUBLISHING LIMITED

First published in 1987 by
Chatto & Windus Ltd

First published in this edition
in the United Kingdom in 1996
Alan Sutton Publishing Ltd
Phoenix Mill
Far Thrupp
Stroud
Gloucestershire

British Library Cataloguing in Publication Data

Harris, Mollie
The Magic of the Cotswold Way.
1. Cotswold Way (England) – Description
and travel
1. Title
914.24'1704858 DA670.C83

ISBN 0-7509-1189-1

Maps drawn by John Flower

Printed in Great Britain by
WBC Limited, Bridgend.

To Beryl,
my daughter-in-law

Who walked with me every step of the Way

Acknowledgements

I would like to thank Bob Arnold, the late Mrs Bostock, Bert and Mabel, 'Gabby' (Gabriel) Clark, Bill Doggett, Joy, Peter and Alan Evans, Mr Ingles, Caroline Elliott, Marion and Harold Greening, the late Victor Haslum, David Harrell, George Hart, Mary Osborn, John Osborne, 'Shackutts', Stanley Sherbourne, Dr Short, lady tramp, Dawn and Des Tomlins, Melvo Taylor, Mr and Mrs Wooldridge (Sen.), Chas Wright.

Special thanks to Harold Greening for snippets of history about Winchcombe, Belas Knap and Hailes; to George Hart for information on Chipping Campden; to Richard Early for information on the woollen mills, and to all my friends and acquaintances, many who I have not named, for all the little bits of local history that have helped to make *The Magic of the Cotswold Way* even more magical. And for tea and tales, lifts and laughs, and for the wonderful help and kindnesses we received from everyone we encountered along the Cotswold Way.

Thank you

Mollie Harris

Contents

List of Illustrations

The old finger post, just over two miles from the start of our walk at Chipping Campden.

A Note on the Cotswold Way

The Cotswold Way follows the line of the escarpment from Chipping Campden to Bath, and is different from most of the long-distance footpaths because it has not been designated by an Act of Parliament, nor opened as a national footpath, but travels along existing rights of way.

The Cotswold Way owes much of its existence to the Gloucestershire Ramblers' Association, who put forward a planned footpath route along the Cotswold escarpment in the early fifties. However, the scheme was not launched until Footpath Week in May 1970.

The marking of the Cotswold Way – using the symbol of an arrow and a white spot – has been carried out by the Cotswold wardens, a group of volunteer workers. In many places there are green signposts pointing to the Cotswold Way: these often have white spots on them, too. But be prepared – occasionally the spots are nonexistent, or covered by bushes and trees. In one place a farmer had renewed his farm gate and gatepost – this foiled us properly until he came out and explained what had happened.

The walk can be enjoyed in every season and by all sorts of people, whether hardened walkers or just casual dawdlers. The Way is an unbroken ridge of high hills and deep valleys, through magical woodlands and open commons, deserted stone quarries and lovely villages. Two things give the Cotswolds their true identity – stone and fleece, fleece and stone: these are all around in what has been described as 'England's wonderland of beauty'.

If you decide to walk any part of this wonderland, do be sure to wear stout footwear and warm but light clothing, and carry waterproofs in your back pack. On one occasion I saw a person floundering about along a muddy track, dressed in a heavy duffle-coat which came way past the knees, a two-yard-long scarf that whipped round and round in the wind, and no stick. No wonder he found it heavy going! No matter what your age, do take either a walking stick or a thumb stick: you will find them a very great benefit.

And I hope that this wondrous countryside gives you as much joy as it gave us.

Mollie Harris

Introduction

On a cold, fine day last February my daughter-in-law, Beryl, and I set out to walk the Cotswold Way, a matter of 100 miles from Chipping Campden to Bath, along the bridleways and footpaths of the Cotswold escarpment – on what was to become a voyage of discovery, a wondrous, magical, never-to-be-forgotten journey. But we didn't keep just to the Cotswold Way: if we spied a village nestling in the valley that we thought looked interesting, we wandered down, often to find a gem of a place, quiet and peaceful, with interesting people living there.

Our great adventure – for that is what it turned out to be – took us about eight months to complete. We walked, on average, about one day every two weeks, setting off very early in the mornings, so that we had completed about six miles by midday. Sometimes we had to retrace our steps to reach the car and the starting-point, other times we hitched rides back and found the folk most kind. Altogether we must have walked at least 160 miles during those eight months.

We wandered through what must be some of the loveliest countryside in Britain, discovering ancient long barrows like Belas Knap and Hetty Pegler's Tump, lovely quiet villages built of mellow stone from nearby quarries, and wild, whispering, wonderful woodlands of beech and oak. The light and shade of leafy valleys, the music of running water and the green slopes of those hills that make up the Cotswolds constantly delighted us.

We discovered abbeys and ancient inns, farmhouses and lonely footpaths, and – most of all – the joy of walking through the changing seasons in the Cotswolds. From high up on those windswept wolds – 'Those high wild hills', as Shakespeare called them – we gazed down at villages and towns in the valleys, with their lofty wool churches towering high above, built by the medieval wool-merchants from the wealth they made from the Cotswold sheep.

The middle part of our journey along the Cotswold Way took us to Painswick and Stroud with their clear, swift-flowing streams which long ago powered dozens of little cloth mills – many of which, alas, are now silent – and then on through breathtaking countryside to the beautiful city of Bath.

But it wasn't only the beautiful scenery and buildings that made our journey so memorable, it was also the wonderful country folk we met along the way. And *you* too can meet some of them as you journey with us and enjoy the magic of the Cotswolds.

ONE

Leave Only Footprints, Take Only Memories

The morning was fine and cold as we set off on our journey to Chipping Campden, which was to be our starting point. We drove via Burford and Stow-on-the-Wold. When we reached the high ground at Stow the mist was so thick that we could only see a few yards in front of us. This, we thought, was not a good beginning, for half the joy of this sort of walk, we hoped, would be the views.

As we turned right off the A44 to Chipping Campden, we noticed the ancient four-hand signpost, one of the few old finger-posts left. Apparently it was erected by Nathaniel Izod in 1699. Should you pass that way, be careful not to miss it: unlike modern signposts it's very tall – so that drivers of the old coaches or horse-riders could read it, no doubt. As we dropped down the steep, winding road to the town the mist suddenly cleared, the sky was a brilliant blue and the pale winter sun was shining on the gilt weather vanes on top of what is said to be the tallest church tower in the Cotswolds (120 feet). The weather vanes – some folk call them wind vanes – looked like banners winking and blinking in the sun, as if to welcome us on our way. 'They've got the flags out for us, I reckon,' I remarked to Beryl.

Much has been written about the history of Chipping Campden, so I shall not write too much about it, except to say that as we wandered down the winding High Street, I thought it was one of the loveliest market towns in the Cotswolds. Chipping Campden's wealth and prosperity, of course, came from the rich wool merchants of the fourteenth and fifteenth centuries – whose monuments are the magnificent wool churches.

The bells of St James's were ringing out as we reached the church and nearby, on a raised pavement, we could see the famous row of alms houses. They were erected in 1612 by a great benefactor to the town, Sir Baptist Hicks, to house six poor women and six poor men. The alms houses are beautifully built of mellow Cotswold stone, with

Map I

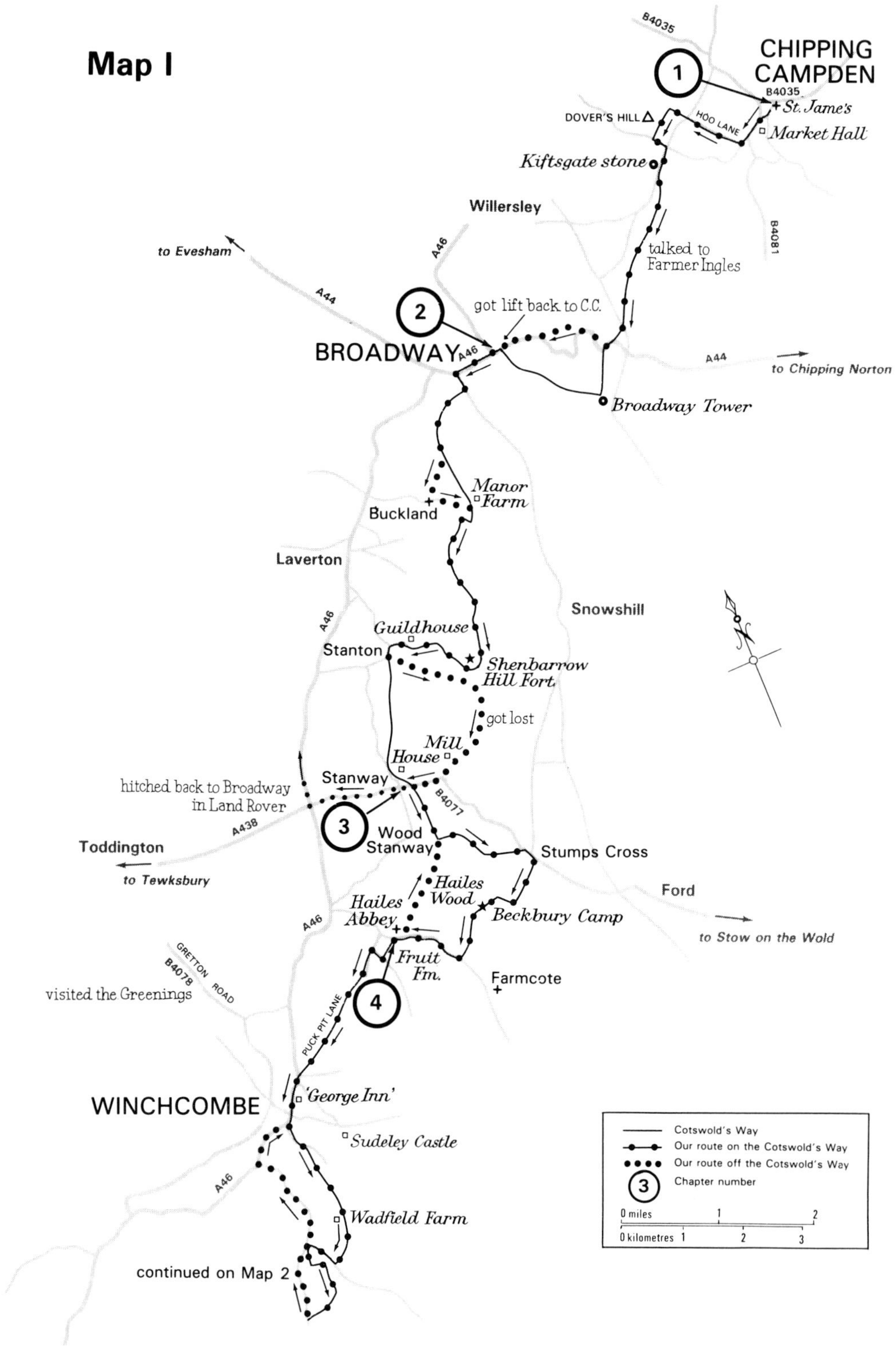

B4035
CHIPPING CAMPDEN
1
B4035
St. James's
Market Hall
DOVER'S HILL
HOO LANE
Kiftsgate stone
Willersley
B4081
to Evesham
A46
talked to Farmer Ingles
A44
2
got lift back to C.C.
BROADWAY
A46
A44
to Chipping Norton
Broadway Tower
Manor Farm
Buckland
Laverton
Snowshill
A46
Guildhouse
Stanton
Shenbarrow Hill Fort
got lost
Mill House
Stanway
hitched back to Broadway in Land Rover
B4077
A438
3
Wood Stanway
Stumps Cross
Toddington
to Tewksbury
Hailes Wood
Ford
Hailes Abbey
Beckbury Camp
A46
to Stow on the Wold
GRETTON ROAD
B4078
Fruit Fm.
Farmcote
visited the Greenings
4
PUCK PIT LANE
WINCHCOMBE
'George Inn'
Sudeley Castle
A46
Wadfield Farm
continued on Map 2
Cotswold's Way
Our route on the Cotswold's Way
Our route off the Cotswold's Way
3
Chapter number
0 miles
1
2
0 kilometres
1
2
3

tall chimneys and lovely mullioned windows. The whole block are built in the shape of the letter I as a mark of respect to King James I. It was here that I had arranged to meet George Hart – Jethro Larkin in *The Archers*.

'Are they ringing for our benefit?' I asked George, smiling.

'No,' he replied, in his lovely Cotswold dialect. ''Tis just bell ringing practice.'

'You are going to tell me a bit about your life here in Campden, aren't you, George?'

'Well, yes, I'll have a go if you thinks that it's interestin' enough for your little book. My father, also named George, came to Chipping Campden from the East End of London in 1901, when C. R. Ashbee brought fifty members of his Guild of Handicrafts and their families here. My old dad was a silversmith, and although some of the members went back to London when the Guild split up in 1909, my father stayed on, married a local farmer's daughter and carried on with his silversmithing, combining it with farming. He was so well known in his day that a letter from America simply addressed to "George Hart, Gloucestershire, England", reached him.

'Well, after attending the local grammar school I served my apprenticeship as a silversmith. I was very good at my job, they said, and after five years was made a Freeman of the Worshipful Company of Goldsmiths and also made a Freeman of the City of London. At the outbreak of World War Two, as a territorial I was called up straight away and went on to serve in most every country where the war was being waged. Somewhere we got hold of an old piano and started our own concert party, and we carted that old jo-anna with us through seven or eight countries. We had some smashing times, as well as some bad ones, especially when we was chasing Rommel all over the desert. I was soon made a captain in the Royal Artillery and finished up as a major at the end of the war.

'Back in civvy street I returned to the family business of silversmithing, but after the outdoor life of the army I couldn't stand working indoors, so I got a job as an area sales manager in an agricultural machinery firm, which took me to the farms and the countryside around. Oh, and I also played hockey and cricket for Campden. I did my first broadcast in 1935, then I joined *The Archers*, and I've played the part of Jethro for the past twenty years. I was given a celebration dinner by the BBC to mark the occasion in February 1985 – being the only member of the cast to have achieved fifty years of radio acting.

'Thankfully, my brother carried on with the silversmithing business, and he and his son still produce lovely, original silverware in their workshops, which are situated in what was an old silk mill in Campden.

'Of course,' George went on, 'Campden has changed quite a bit over the years. Oh, I don't mean the architecture, but conditions.'

'In what way?' I asked him.

'Well, street lighting for a start. I remember when it was as black as pitch some nights down the streets in the wintertime. There was very little light from the cottage windows, and it was that damned cold here that most folk drawed the curtains over their windows to help to keep the cottages warm. Well, one winter's night – ah, I must have been about seventeen at the time – I was walking down Campden High Street carrying me lantern, when I met old Charlie Dyer. "Wur be you awf to, young man?" he asked. "I be going down to the hall to give 'um a bit of a song, there's a social on there tonight," I told him. "Well, you don't need a lantern for that, do you?" "Ah," I replied, "I might do a bit of courting afterwards." "Well, you certainly don't want a lantern for that job, do 'ee? I never 'ad one when I went courting me missus." "Ah," I replied, "one look at her and I can tell that you didn't."

'Oh, we had some rare characters living here years ago,' George went on, 'and in the villages around. One old fellow known hereabouts as Jim Jam Smith, come from Blockley he did, and he was a bit peculiar. Somebody met him one day and asked him how he was. "Ah, I don't rightly know," he said. "What do you mean?" the fellow asked. "Well," Jim Jam replied, "I ain't seen the *Evesham Journal* yet." "What the devil's that got to do with it?" asked this bloke. "Well, when the paper comes, I reads down all the names in the death column, and if my name yent thur I knaws I be all right."

George Hart and Mollie: 'Are the bells ringing for us?' I asked.

'But old age is creeping on, I got arthritis in my feet that bad. But I do so much enjoy playing in *The Archers*, and I hope I can go on for a long time yet. And I likes me pint at the local, where we has a good laugh and joke. Did I tell you the one about the traveller, lost he was, well it was late at night, there was nobody about, but then he spies a light in Fred Thacket's window. So he goes up the path, knocks on the door. Fred answered it and asked the stranger, "What do yer want at this time of night?" Stuttering a bit the man said, "Could you tell me the right way to Campden, please?" Fred, always John Blunt, said, "If you be going that way you a' passed it, but if you be facing t'other way you be just coming to it" – and slammed the door.'

What a character! We could have listened all day to George's tales. But enough of this – we must get on our way and start walking!

So we thanked George, said cheerio, and made our way down the famous High Street, past William Grevel's house which was built during the fourteenth century: a lovely building with its Gothic doorway, fine stonework and a perpendicular bay window. It is reputed to have been the first house in Chipping Campden to have chimneys rather than vents in the roof, to carry the smoke away. William Grevel was a wool merchant and a very successful one, too, and in the Church of St James – of which he was one of the most prominent benefactors – a huge memorial brass to him states that he was 'the flower of the wool merchants of all England'.

From there we walked on past the beautiful mellow Jacobean Market Hall, which was built in 1627 by Sir Baptist Hicks at the cost of £90, and was first used by farmers' wives as a shelter under which they sold their butter, eggs and cheeses. In the High Street every house and cottage has its own unique style, built in warm honey-coloured stone by craftsmen who lived in the prosperous era when the 'Cotswold Lions' – as the huge Cotswold sheep were sometimes called – roamed the hills in their thousands and brought much wealth and work to the area.

We reached the end of the street and started to look for a sign to Hoo Lane and the Cotswold Way. The sign was marked with an arrow and the white spot which denote a Cotswold Waymark – and one which we would come to rely on during our long walk. Our goal was Broadway, about five miles away as the crow flies. As we left Hoo Lane behind us we could just see the famous Broadway Tower over to our left, and it seemed miles and miles away.

It had been raining overnight, and since the lane, besides being a right of way for walkers, is also a farm track, the ruts that the tractors had made were a foot deep in places. Of course we were well kitted-out with walking gear and we carried our thumb sticks. These proved to be most helpful during the coming months, and I for one would never have made it during some of the very steep and heavy walking that we encountered, had it not been for the help that thumb stick gave me. You use them as you would a walking stick, and they help to lever you along. My old shepherd friend, Mont Abbott, had specially cut both Beryl's and mine. When I told him that we were off on this long walk he said, 'Ah, theet waunt a good thumb stick apiece, I'll cut 'e a hazel or a blackthorn one.'

For a while the going was quite hard, then we crossed a road and turned up another track which wasn't too bad. We were puffing and blowing at the steepness, for we had been climbing steadily ever since we had made our way up Hoo Lane. We turned and looked back on the town of Campden below: we must have climbed a hundred feet or more, and were level with those famous gilded weather vanes on top of the church tower.

In one field several women were busy, backs bent picking Brussels sprouts; rather them than me, I thought, for the wind was quite cold up there. It's one thing to be striding along for the joy of it, and another to be working up there all day. In another field, men were cutting down what looked to be plum trees. We found out later that some growers were getting rid of a particular type of plum that is not very popular these days with the housewife.

By the time we had reached Dover's Hill, a mile or more out of Campden, the weather had changed – there was a gale-force wind blowing, and we could hardly hear ourselves speak for the wind rushing and roaring through the bare branches of the giant beech trees. We were glad to walk a little way down the hill – although this was not the way we were going – to seek shelter from the gale. The view over the Vale of Evesham was beautiful, and we could see for miles and miles – to the Malvern Hills and beyond. It really was quite breathtaking. In a few weeks' time it will be even more spectacular – the Vale will be covered with plum blossom, and will look like a great sea of white foam. Dover's Hill – now deserted save for us and a man walking his dog – was once a very busy spot, for this was where Captain Robert Dover founded the 'Cotswold Olympicks' in the early seventeenth century. The games consisted of those sports that were most popular at that time – wrestling, leaping, single-stick, throwing the iron hammer, sword-play, shin-kicking and something called cudgel-bar fighting. The games were held once a year at Whitsuntide and went on until 1852 when they were barred because they were thought too rowdy. But they were revived in 1951 and are now held on the eve of the Scuttlebrook wake, on the Saturday following the spring bank holiday. The name Scuttlebrook is derived from the 'cattle brook', an open stream that once ran through the east end of Chipping Campden, called Leysbourne. The stream was eventually diverted under the town. Scuttlebrook wake or fair is now held on the green verge of Leysbourne on the Saturday following the spring bank holiday when, as well as the fun fair, there is a procession of dressed vehicles and fancy dress in the streets, and children's races.

To guide us on our way we were armed with a small green booklet called *The Cotswold Way*, quite well marked but not in great detail, and – after losing our way a few times – we learned later that we should really carry an Ordnance Survey map. Later we bought one and found it most useful, as it gave details of fields and paths.

We left Dover's Hill and, keeping to the signs, we then had to walk along the road for a while. 'We must look out for the Kiftsgate Stone,' I said. 'It's supposed to be along here, on the right, in a little spinney quite close to the road – well, so the book says anyhow.'

We entered the spinney and made our way through a lot of blackberry brambles and began to search around. 'Here it is!' I cried, spying a stone about three feet high set very firmly in the ground. This stone is said to mark the meeting place of the Kiftsgate Hundred in Saxon times, where the people of the surrounding district met to discuss important matters, and the kings of England were proclaimed from it. We were just about to take a photo of it when a car stopped a few yards from us and a man got out.

'Good Lord,' said Beryl, 'surely he's not going to grumble at us for being here?' The man, a farmer by his clothes, grinned at us.

'Looking at our famous stone then?' he asked cheerfully. We told him of our intended walk, and discovered that he was on his way to look at his flock of sheep that were in a field about a mile away, close to the Cotswold Way. Here was someone that I'd like to have a chat with about keeping sheep up there on those 'high wild hills and rough uneven ways', as Shakespeare described the Cotswolds in *Richard III.*

'Can I give you a lift?' he asked.

'Oh, no,' we replied. 'We are *walking* the Cotswold Way. We might be glad to cadge a lift back to the car some time, but *not* on the *outward* journey,' we told him firmly.

The Kiftsgate Stone, from which the kings of England were proclaimed.

So he promised to wait for us with his flock until we reached his fields.

We had dressed for winter, but were already sweating. We stopped to remove a layer of woollies which we stuffed in our back packs. Country workers always set off in suitable clothes: you can always take clothes off if you get too hot, but there's nothing worse than working out in a field all day inadequately dressed – and the same applies to walkers.

The trees were still quite bare, but then it was early February. High above, the skylarks were singing – which reminded me of one of John Masefield's poems, which goes 'On Campden Wold the Skylark Sings'. By the time we took our next walk some of the buds on the trees and hedgerows might well be showing.

We could see the farmer, Mr Ingles, waiting for us a little way in front. It was still blowing a gale, so he suggested we sat in the car for our chat.

'Well,' he said, 'I was born and brought up at our home called Whitehouse Farm in the lovely village of Willersey just down in the valley, and I lived at the farm with my family until I was twenty-one.

'When I was ten years old, I used to have to walk into Chipping Campden to school, a matter of three miles each way. I used to cut across the fields when it was dry enough. On one of the field gates there was a notice "Beware of adders" – I didn't half leg it across that field, I can tell you.

'Just before I got married I decided to strike out on my own. I had the chance to rent thirty acres of land that was already planted with fruit trees, because, of course, Willersey is in the Vale of Evesham and a wonderful growing area for hard and soft fruits and all kinds of vegetables. But that very first year I took over was disastrous for all the growers in the Vale of Evesham – well, as far as their crops of plums and apples were concerned – because that was the year of the terrible frosts. 1930, it was. The frosty weather lasted throughout February until March, I saw old fellows break down and cry when they saw the damage to the crops and fruit blossom – it was that bad. But, strangely enough, that year everyone – including myself – who had grown cherries had the most wonderful crop. I suppose the blossom bloomed soon after the thaw. I remember taking mine into Evesham market – and I got a very good price for them, too. And the following summer was an extremely hot one.

'A bit later I got married. My wife and I worked very hard growing gooseberries, raspberries and strawberries, as well as the hard fruits.

'Then the family came along – three boys and one daughter. All the boys are interested in farming and market gardening. We keep a fairly big flock of sheep, and beef cattle which we fatten up and sell. As the family got married and left home, we found that the house was far too big so we had what was once the cart shed, a lovely Cotswold stone building, turned into what we think is a very attractive conversion. We are very happy and contented there, and are still living in the pleasant village of Willersey, surrounded by our family and friends.'

The interview over, Mr Ingles said, 'Would you like to come down to the farm at Willersey and have a cup of coffee? The wife would be

Mr and Mrs Ingles at home: 'We are very happy and contented here.'

most pleased to see you – and,' he went on, nodding in my direction, 'she's a proper Archer fan.' We declined his kind offer, for time was getting on and we had to make our way to Broadway.

After walking for about a mile we stopped for a bite to eat, sitting in the 'burra', or shelter, of a lovely Cotswold wall. With the pale sun shining on our faces we ate our cheese sandwiches and shared a bottle of fruit juice. Caviare and champagne could not have tasted as wonderful as did that, our first meal of the walk – one of many that we were to enjoy in the open air over the next few months.

Either we were not looking where we were going, or the Way marking was not too good, but we got lost twice before snaking our way down Broadway Hill. Not on the road, mind you! Oh, no! Still on springy grass: the path ran almost parallel with the road, all downhill, and the going was easy. We reached our goal – the green at Broadway – at about 2.30 p.m. *and* still had to make our way back to Chipping Campden and the car before dark.

Cotswold stone wallers.

George Hart had told me about an old fellow who lives in Broadway to whom I would probably like to talk. His name was Clark, George told me – 'Some folks calls him Clark Gable, some calls him Gabby and some Gabriel, but if you gets the chance to have a word with him you'll find him most interesting. A bit of a poacher, he is,' he added.

'How shall I find him?' I enquired.

'When you gets to the green, look out for a fellow in a trilby hat, a long brown coat and a ferret in his pocket,' he said. After a while we found the very man, and made arrangements to have a chat to him on the next leg of our walk. 'You ring the landlord of The Crown and Trumpet,' Gabby said, 'he'll give me a message any time.'

Now for the journey back. The sun had disappeared, the wind was quite cold and it was getting late. We asked about buses but none were going to Campden.

'I'm not legging it up that damned long hill,' I told Beryl, 'the next car that comes along I shall stick my thumb out' – and I did. The first car which stopped contained an elderly couple, and we told them of our plight. 'Jump in,' they said, not minding our muddy boots and cumbersome sticks and knapsacks. We tumbled thankfully into the car – until then we hadn't realised how tired we were. They took us right to where we had parked the car. We tried to tell them how very grateful we were – but I doubt if they will ever realise *how* grateful.

We drove home, happy but very weary. The first leg of our adventure was over, and we were eagerly looking forward to our next walk.

TWO

As Sure as God's in Gloucestershire

It was early March before we had the chance to set off over the Cotswold hills again, but at least the weather had, by now, turned bright and clear, though the wind blew cold in unsheltered places.

We had arranged to meet Gabby at ten o'clock on the green at Broadway. He was there waiting for us, his weather-beaten face so wrinkled and red that it resembled a russet apple in autumn, and he grinned a half-toothless grin when he spotted us.

'You haven't brought your ferret today, have you?' I asked him.

'No, ma'am, not today. I've left 'im at 'ome, I only brings 'im out when I be going to do me a bit of poachin', yu see.'

Early springtime in Broadway – like any other time in this popular village – was quite busy with tourists, but we did manage to find ourselves an empty seat.

'Right, then,' I said. 'What do I call you – Gabby, Gabriel or Clark Gable?'

He laughed – I would think that in his younger days he had been a very attractive man.

'Call me Gabby,' he said, 'nearly everybody else do.' He went on, 'Well, I've always lived in Broadway, born and brought up there I was. You see, my old dad was postman here, and in them days they had to walk everywhere to deliver the post. His area wasn't in Broadway, but all round the little villages and outlying farms, and sometimes when the weather was bad and the snow was four or five feet deep along the roads, he was often trapped in some of them lonely villages. Folk used to put him up for the night, and he often had to sleep on an old sofa or in a couple of chairs. Folks had big families then, so they wouldn't have had a proper bed to spare. In them days the postman had to empt the letter boxes in the villages and take the letters back to Broadway, and if the folks hadn't got a stamp they would wait on their doorstep for my father to walk into their village,

'Gabby' Clarke at Broadway, grinning a toothless grin.

and he would sell them a stamp or two. If a person couldn't wait for him to arrive, they would post the unstamped letter in the post box along with the coppers to pay for the stamp.

''Course, half of our living he caught, 'cos he was a poacher, too. What he did was set his traps for hares and rabbits in the morning on his way out to the villages, and call in the afternoons to pick up his catches. He would paunch the animals there and then out on the grass, and put his "game" in his letter bag. Ah! many a person had an unexpected "red letter" where the blood used to get all over them.'

'But what about you and your life here in Broadway?' I asked.

'Well, I'm a bit of a rebel really. I likes to live me own life me own way. Once I shot a hawk and hung him up on a stick and string in me garden to try and scare the birds off me peas, and a neighbour reported me and said that I had hung up that hawk before he was dead, and that his wings was a-flapping for a long while. They took me to court for it anyway. And the magistrate fined me three pounds

– but I told him I hadn't got that amount of money. Then I was asked how much I could afford to pay a week, and I said sixpence, so that was how I paid it off.

'Anytime,' Gabby went on, 'that you be along this way and you wants a pheasant for dinner, you just come along and see old Gabby – I'll get you one from somewhere.'

It was true, too. George Hart had told me that if Gabby was in a pub, and someone told him that they wanted a pheasant or a couple of partridges, he would slip out and return about an hour later with a still warm bird.

I thanked Gabby for giving me his time, and said that we ought to be getting a move on. Then, very politely, he said, 'Would you two young ladies' – that made my day – 'like to come and have a drink along'a me at The Crown and Trumpet?' We said no, but would he have one on us? We had quite a long way to go and we had already dallied too long on the green at Broadway in the welcome winter sunshine.

So, without looking at our guide book, we set off along the road out of Broadway towards Evesham. We could see the Cotswold ridge high up on our left, and we knew that was where we had to get to. 'There must be a footpath sign along here somewhere,' I said. We were almost out of the village, with just a few houses on our right. A woman was backing her car out of her drive, so we asked her if we were going in the right direction to get onto the Cotswold Way. 'No, my dears, you are certainly not. Look, you jump in the car and I'll take you back to the starting point.' We chatted excitedly as she drove along, telling her of our plan to walk the entire Cotswold Way.

'Hope you don't mind me saying,' she said, addressing me, 'but your voice is very familiar – are you Martha in *The Archers*?' I nodded.

'Then you are Mollie Harris in real life, aren't you? I've read all your books. I feel I know all about you.' She was so pleased to think that she had not only met, but also given a lift to, a member of the cast of her favourite programme. ''Course, when I read your first book *A Kind of Magic*,' she went on, 'I realised that it was my parents who bought Mill Farm at Sherbourne from your cousins, the Broads, before they went on to Home Farm at Upper Slaughter.' It's a small world – there we were, two complete strangers, and yet we had stopped and asked the way from someone whose parents had bought my relation's farm, where I used to stay as a child after my grandparents had died.

Our friend went on: 'Here you are, this is where you start. When you get near to Buckland – that's the next little village you'll see down in the valley, about a mile or so from here on your right – well, if you've got time go down into the village, it won't take you long, and have a look at the beautiful church, and the fifteenth-century rectory, which is supposed to be the oldest one in England still in use.'

She left us with a promise to listen to any broadcasts that I might do about the walk.

We set off briskly, soon reaching a roughish path, and after climbing steadily for a while we spied the village of Buckland in the valley, and decided to visit it – it was downhill all the way, and we literally ran down the grassy hillside. And what a delightful place it turned out to be. The church was lovely, with unusual canopied seating. What intrigued me was the sixteenth-century Buckland bowl which, at one time, was used as a loving cup at weddings: it is made of maple wood with silver around the edge, and I have never seen anything like it before. Apparently the rectory is sometimes open to the public, but not on this day, so we shall have to pay it a visit some other time.

Now for the climb back! We wondered whether there might be another route up to the ridge and decided to ask a man who was busy cutting his lawn.

'Oh, yes,' he replied, 'just up the lane here, then turn right into a field, and then *left*, and that will take you up there.'

We did as he said, walked down the lane, turned right into a field climbing steeply all the while, and then we saw a very worn path on our *right*.

'This looks like the way,' Beryl said, and we started along it.

Suddenly a shout from down in the valley made us turn round sharpish. It was our grass-cutting friend, who from his garden had been keeping his weather eye on us. He was waving his arms and shouting, 'Go left, left, left.' We waved back, feeling a bit foolish, then turned on our heels and took the less worn path to the left. Sure enough it took us to a stile where the Way was clearly signposted; then on and on, climbing up steeply through a farm. We took a last look at our gardening friend, waved, and puffed our way back onto the ridge. We noticed on our walk up that a few of the trees and bushes were starting to show their leaf buds – the elder and sycamore seemed most advanced, and the flowers of the coltsfoot (pee-the-beds, we always called them when we were young), and celandines and ground ivy were out, too. In a little copse we saw a few early wood anemones or wind flowers, as some people call them – flowers that don't open until the winds blow high. Folklore tells us that they close up tight at night because woodland fairy folk sleep in them.

We passed a couple of stone quarries, and a glance at the book told us that we were almost a thousand feet up Shenberrow hillfort, an Iron Age construction. Nearby was a footpath signpost. To the left was the village of Snowshill, with its beautiful Cotswold stone manor house dating back to 1500 or so. Now owned by the National Trust, the house is filled with curios and the terraced gardens are massed with old-fashioned roses and shrubs, and are certainly worth a visit. Not as famous as the manor but still worth a mention is the fact that in 1842 Charles Keyte of Snowshill invented a sewing machine, which is now in the Science Museum.

But the path we took went straight ahead, for our goal was the beautiful village of Stanton, which we soon glimpsed in the valley below – after which we hoped to walk on to Stanway. The going now was all downhill, through a small wood and fields. Soon we reached Stanton, quiet and peaceful in the early afternoon pale sunshine. The village was bought by the architect Sir Philip Stott, who owned the estate from 1906 to 1927, and was beautifully restored by him. We peeped in at the twelfth-century church where John Wesley often preached, and saw the old oak benches streaked with grooves. These were made by dog chains: apparently, many years ago shepherds took their dogs along with them and tied them to the pew ends when they went to worship there. I had heard of a lady who, some years ago, had founded a guildhouse which is built on the side of a hill in the village, and I hoped to have a chat to her about it.

We saw an elderly man out walking with his dog, so we asked him where the guildhouse was.

'Just up there – look on that hill.'

And there it was in front of us, 'a poem in stone', as someone called it. We could hardly believe that this lovely mellow Cotswold building, solid and traditional, set in the hillside of this delightful village, was, in fact, less than twenty years old. We went in and met Miss Osborn, whose dream it was to build this lovely guildhouse.

I asked her how it all began.

'Many years ago I did social work in London,' she told me, 'and I thought how wonderful it would be if I could set up a kind of guildhouse where people of all denominations, black or white, rich or poor, male or female, and of any age, could go to some safe refuge in a quiet, peaceful place, to renew their hopes, and perhaps learn the age-old, simple crafts of weaving, spinning, woodwork, pottery, and the like.

'At first I lived in a small cottage at the nearby village of Laverton. The children there knew that I did spinning and weaving, and they used to bring me handfuls of sheep's wool that they had collected from brambles and barbed wire in the local fields. Many of these children showed a great interest in what I was doing, and in time some of them learned to spin and weave. I was convinced more than ever that there was a great need for some place where people could learn the gentle arts.

'Well, first of all, after much searching, this plot of ground was found. A benefactor bought it for us and gave £1000 to start us off. Someone else offered us the stone from five old Cotswold stone barns if we could get it hauled away. Five hundred and fifty tons of it was brought here and used in the building of the guildhouse.

'Of course this was a great help, but much, much more help and money was needed. I have sat on the steps of St Paul's in London working my spinning wheel to try and encourage people to help us

Mollie talking to Mary Osborne at the Guildhouse.

with the building of the guildhouse, and I have done the same thing in Stratford-upon-Avon market place, too. The building work, which took over ten years to complete, was mostly done by student volunteers. From all over the world they came, year after year, and worked under the guidance of two skilled craftsmen.'

Inside the large, roomy hall there were several ladies spinning; all around were examples of pottery, and lovely hand-woven curtains hung gracefully at the windows.

I noticed the old-fashioned wooden door latches and Miss Osborn said, 'Yes, they were a gift to the house, all made by a disabled man.' They were beautiful and, I think, will last for ever.

'Don't forget to have a look in at the woodworkers,' Miss Osborn said, as we made to leave.

We made our way to the woodworking room. There were four or five men and an instructor, busily making all sorts of things. They came there for one afternoon a week. Beryl said, as we walked away,

'I've never seen such happy men before.'

I was only in Miss Osborn's presence for about an hour, but even so I came away refreshed and uplifted. This is how the whole atmosphere of the guildhouse and its creator makes you feel.

Very reluctantly we left the quiet, peaceful guildhouse, and walked on through the village. On the outskirts we saw the now familiar footpath sign with its white spot, which directed us along the edge of a field. We climbed over a stile and into the next field, and met coming towards us a group of walkers whom we had seen earlier in the day. They were evidently doing the same walk as us, only the other way round. We stopped and chatted for a few minutes – the men admiring our thumb sticks. Since some of their party were in the valley, while others were halfway down the hill, we naturally thought that the path led over the hill. Up and up we went – it was very hard going, and I had to stop a couple of times to get my second wind. Beryl struggled on in front, and even she was making heavy going of it.

The sky had become cloudy – it was about six o'clock, and it was beginning to get dimpsey. Beryl started to panic. 'We're lost,' she cried, 'and we'll be up here all night if we're not careful.'

She started to walk back towards Stanton. 'No!' I cried, 'you're going back to where we came from, we have to go in this direction.'

So we set off again, and after a while came to what looked like an old mill. There were a few lorries about but no drivers. We continued down the narrow road, at least it was all downhill, so we were walking quite fast – and then, thankfully, we came into Stanway. Then, after we had spotted a footpath sign, we realised that we should have stayed in the valley when we met the walkers – and that if we had, we shouldn't have had that awful struggle up the grass hill, or have got lost on top of it!

Anyway, we had a good laugh about it. I suppose it was the relief of knowing where we were, and realising what idiots we had been.

Still, we were in Stanway and even though it was early March the whole place was covered with snowdrops. They were blooming everywhere, in every garden, every grass verge, in the orchards and even at the base of the hedgerows. I've never seen such a display in my life – they were absolutely lovely. Of course, we couldn't help but notice the beautiful and very famous gatehouse leading to Stanway House. Historians once believed that it was the work of Inigo Jones, but now many say it is more likely to have been the work of Timothy Strong, a Cotswold master stone-mason from Little Barrington. Stanway House is a marvellous Jacobean manor house which is sometimes open to the public. And beyond is the huge tithe barn that was built around 1370: once it was used to store grain and other harvests, but now serves as a magnificent hall for flower shows and the like. All this and a cluster of cottages all built in warm honey-coloured stone, make up what must be one of the most lovely and unspoiled villages in the Cotswolds.

'How shall we get back to Broadway?' Beryl asked. 'There'll never be time to retrace our steps over the fields – it would be dark before we got there.'

'I know,' I said brightly. 'We might just see a notice in a cottage window that says "Taxi for hire" – we'll get back that way.' What a hope – we saw nothing of the kind!

'Well, there's nothing else for it. We shall have to leg it back,' I said, and we set off at a goodly pace up the road that would eventually bring us out on the main Winchcombe–Broadway road. But we were both getting tired – we must have walked at least eight miles already, and our pace was getting slower and slower. Several cars came towards us, but not one from behind!

'When a vehicle does come up behind us,' I said, 'I shall thumb it down. I don't care what it is – even a ride on a tractor would be welcome.'

After we had trudged along for another three-quarters of a mile, a Land Rover came whizzing along. I stuck my thumb out and, joy of joys, the driver pulled up. We told him where we wanted to get to. 'Hop in the back,' he said, cheerfully. So we clambered in along with a couple of friendly collie dogs, and several tins of one thing and another.

'Sorry there's no room in the front,' he said. On the seat beside him were a couple of sacks of sheep nuts. We learned as we sped along that he was shepherd for the local squire and hadn't intended to go to Broadway before he saw us.

'I was really only going to the next field to feed the sheep when I picked you up, but you both looked so woebegone, I knew that you weren't used to hiking. Normally I never pick anyone up,' he went on, 'my boss wouldn't think too much of it, anyway.'

He took us right to the car park in Broadway.

What splendid people we had met that day! As we drove home, we decided that we must get a field map before we set out again – our experiences today had made us realise that – and that we must sit down and plan just where we were going, for we had lost a lot of unnecessary time and energy. A walk like this is not something to be taken lightly, and, according to the little green book, we had some very lonely and hard walking to do later on!

THREE

Apples, Rams and Cider

By now we had become full of enthusiasm about the walk, and we eagerly looked forward to the next trip, which would take us to Wood Stanway, Stumps Cross and on to Hailes. So we parked the car on the vergeside in Stanway – the village where we had finished our walk last time.

Wood Stanway is a little hamlet of just a few cottages and farms. The Way was quite well marked – according to the guide book, when we reached the hamlet we were to turn left just after one of the farms and come to a row of cottages, which we were to leave on our right. Standing outside one of the cottages was a homely looking woman.

'Lost yer way, have you?' she called out.

We walked towards her and away from the footpath sign.

'I'm always showing people the way,' she went on, 'they gets as far as here and they ent quite sure whether they should come past here or go on up the lane where the sign is. You can really please yourself,' she went on, 'you can cut the corner off and go straight across this field and up into Hailes Wood, or follow the sign which will take you up to Stumps Cross, and eventually to Hailes Wood. You'll end up in the same place – Hailes Abbey – anyway. Why don't you come in and have a bit of a set down?' she said.

We had only just started, but she seemed such a friendly body we couldn't refuse. Her name, we learned, was Mrs Bostock, a widow woman, and she was so pleased to have someone to talk to. She was born in the cottage where she lived, and so was her father, and her grandfather who had brought his young bride of seventeen there after being married at Stanway church. They had had twelve or thirteen children – she wasn't quite sure.

We remarked on the lovely peaceful setting.

'Oh, yes,' she said, 'it's a lot quieter than it used to be. When I was a youngster there were about thirty children here, 'course they always had big families in them days. We played outside all summer long, and was quite contented.

'Mind you, we used to get up to a lot of tricks, too,' she went on. 'See that big stone out there on the grass? Well, that's the old water supply and where we all used to get our water from. It comes from a lovely spring right up there on the Cotswold ridge, and it's the most beautiful water, too. You can see where the tap used to be, and carved on the stone are the letters QVDJ – Queen Victoria's Diamond Jubilee – it was erected to commemorate that event. I suppose before that the folk used to get the water from the spring as it ran down the hillside . . . Well, what I be getting at is one of the tricks that we played. When we knew that it was going to be a sharp frost we'd whisper to one of our older brothers, "When you goes out to the privy last thing, don't forget to turn the tap on." 'Course, in the morning the lane all along here in front of the cottages was a big sheet of ice, and lovely for us children to slide on. Another thing we used to do was ride the rams.'

'Ride the rams?' I enquired.

'Yes, you see the estate kept ever such a big flock of sheep and six rams as well. Well, when they rams was "resting" the shepherd always put them out in that field over there, and he used to strap leather blindfolds on them to stop them fighting amongst theirselves. As soon as we noticed that they was out in the field, we'd run indoors and ask our mother for some bag-tying string, 'course she didn't know what we was going to get up to, or she'd never given us it. Well, we'd plait the string together and make ourselves stirrups and reins, and harness them rams up and cock our legs over their backs, and ride 'um like donkeys. 'Course they'd rush about all over the field, bumping into trunks of the apple trees, 'cos they couldn't see where they was going. We used to go flying off their backs, but we didn't care, we'd jump on again thundering around the field like cowboys – oh, we did have such fun.

'One day, when we was out there a-shrieking and laughing and riding them rams, suddenly I felt a heavy hand on my shoulder, it was the farmer and he was furious. "Come on down to the farm," he said,

Mrs Bostock and Mollie at the water pump, Wood Stanway.

"come on, all of you," he bellowed – my sisters were hanging back, you see. "I'm going to send for the police," he shouted, "I'll put a stop to this." Oh, we was that frightened. He lined us up in his yard and didn't he tell us off. But he never fetched the police. Mind you, he told our mam and dad and didn't we get a good hiding when we got home – hidings lasted all day in our house, it wasn't just one good 'un and finish – oh, no, every time you went by our mother she'd take a whack at you with her stick – a thin stick it was and she kept it up on the bacon rack. You knows them bacon racks that was fixed up near the ceiling, just above the fireplace, and the sides of bacon from our pig was kept up there in the dry. Well, that's where she kept that stick of 'ers, and we hated it.

'Our mother used to keep bees too – talked to 'um she did. It was a funny thing they never stung her, she could take the top off the hives and get the honey out and she never got stung. But if I or my dad went down to the bottom of the garden to the old privy, I'll bet you some of them bees would follow. I was frightened to death of 'um, but of course I couldn't stay down there too long – as soon as I stuck my head out that old door, ping, one or two would sting me. And our dad was just the same. Our mother used to say that bees was very intelligent things, they must have been, 'cos they knew me and my dad didn't like 'um.

'She had a row of them beehives right down the bottom of the garden, and she used to plant ever such a lot of sweet-smelling flowers down there 'specially for the bees. One day I went down there to pick a big bunch to take to old Mrs Brown who wasn't very well, *and* got stung – that was it, I got a damned good hiding, all day that lasted. "Them flowers be planted for the bees' benefit," she told me, "and not to give away to every Tom, Dick and Harry."

''Course she used to sell the honey, that was the only way she could earn a bit of money, because I expect my dad's wages was only about eighteen shillings a week. 'Course, childlike, we was always doing something as we shouldn't.

'Every day we children was sent up to the farm to get the milk in a blue enamelled can with a handle on and a lid like a cup. Really that can was used for taking tea out to our dad when he was working up in the fields. Our mother would say to us, "Now you go up the lane and come back that way – no scooting across into that orchard," she knew that we loved to get in there and play.

'On this particular Saturday, besides getting the milk, we had to buy half a pound of real dairy butter – not that we had that very often. You see we had an aunt coming to visit us on the Sunday, and this butter from the farm was a special treat for all our tea – lovely that butter was, and the colour of the buttercups out in the fields.

'Well, it was a nice hot day and on our way back we cut through the orchard. Up the top end was ever such a big old stump of a tree, oh, about three feet high. It was hollow, and we loved to play in there. Anyhow, as it was so hot we stood the can of milk and the half pound of butter inside the tree trunk in the cool. Then we played all sorts of games out on the grass, and it was lovely. How long we was up there goodness only knows, but suddenly there was a shouting and a hollering coming from just outside our cottage. It was our mother.

'We went to get the milk and butter – well, you knows the old saying "running like butter in the sun"! It was doing just that, nothing but a yellow patch of grease. By goy, didn't we get it! Good hidings all round all day we had for that.

'But our mother always taught us to be polite and to respect other people. But sometimes I finds that a bit hard to do. You see we gets all sorts passing along here, walking over the hills, and most folk like yourselves are nice ordinary people. But some – not many, mind you – tries to put their talk on. "Crackin' thur jaw" we used to call it – you know, them highfalutin sort. Well, I can't stand 'um, all I does is just tell 'em the way and then goes in and shuts the door. I've mixed with all types of folk in my lifetime and can converse with lords and ladies, rich or poor, but I can't be doing with snobs.'

We both agreed with her, and let her go on.

'And see that big orchard out there? Well, all the workers was allowed so many trees each – and a lot of them bares cider apples. Up there in one of the buildings there is a great big old cider press so everybody had the chance to make their own cider. Some of the men would be drinking it all Sunday morning and by dinner time they was as drunk as fiddlers.

'At one time a cowman used to live just a few doors away in what we've always called the Drovers' Cottage, 'cos years ago when the drovers brought their cattle up this way from Wales, that cottage was where the men would sleep overnight. Well, this 'ere cowman used to get terrible drunk, so one day when he'd gone to work his wife turned on the tap of the big barrel of cider that he'd made and it all run down the path and into the little stream out there. He was hopping mad when he found out, and threatened to kill her. You see, what really annoyed her was that during the night he used to do a bucketful of pee and in the morning she had to empt it.

'That path that you come along from Stanway used to be called Church Path,' she went on, 'and the workers on the estate had to hoe and tidy that path every othering day so that the ladies could walk along it without getting thurselves all wet or muddy, 'cos they still all wore long black skirts, you see. We had to walk along that path to school,' Mrs Bostock went on, 'but that has been closed for a long while now. The gentry from the big house are most kind and good to their workers. It's a champion place to live, I got hens out in the orchard, as much wood as I wants for me fire, a good long garden full up with stuff – I don't suppose I'd be contented anywhere else.'

We could have stayed chattering all day long, but we had to get on. But we did say that we might see her on the way back, for Beryl and I had already planned to walk to Hailes and back that day.

She came to the door to see us off, and almost at once we started to climb up the steep pathway and finally reached Stumps Cross, which is reputed to be the remains of a medieval cross. What a difference in the countryside the past few weeks had made – green corn shooting up in the fields, clumps of green, ferny leaves of cow parsley, hares and rabbits galore, blackthorn blossom on the hedgerows and dozens of skylarks singing high above. It was a lovely fresh spring day, the sun was quite warm, and we had to shed our thick anoraks for thinner ones. We reached a signpost which stated that it was three kilometres to Hailes. We reached Beckbury Camp, an old hillfort, and climbed to the top. The view was breathtakingly beautiful from so high up, and over the vale clouds of white plum blossom bloomed in the valley.

Mrs Bostock had told us to look out for a big stone seat, supposedly the one on which Thomas Cromwell sat and watched Hailes Abbey burn. 'My initials are carved on there,' she said. We found the stone seat, taking turns to sit on it to have our photos taken, and then made our way towards Hailes. At this point we would have liked to have turned off and made our way to Farmcote to see the tiny church of St Faith's – we thought we might just do that on our way back, depending on the time.

We were walking through a wood when Beryl said, 'I don't think that we're on the right path.' She scanned the field map. 'I think we'd better get out of here before someone catches us.' We reached the edge of the wood and she scrabbled under a wire fence. I tried to do the same: somehow I got caught up in the wire and the force of me

We finally reached Stumps Cross.

trying to get through dislodged my back pack, which was not really on my back at the time but hung over one shoulder. Well, I got through the fence, but the pack went one way and I the other, rolling down the steep grassy bank in the bargain. We sat on the grass and laughed till we were helpless. 'If only I'd had the camera at the ready,' Beryl said, tears running down her cheeks. In fact, we seemed to laugh at a lot of things. It was so wonderful up there, no worries, no cares – just us and the skylarks.

Soon we reached the narrow road and began to walk towards the Abbey. All along there were hundreds of young frogs – many had been run over, but others were crossing over from one side of the road to the other, and then into a damp field.

A Land Rover came along and stopped to let us pass. We remarked on the lovely fresh air. The driver grinned. 'If you want plenty of that,' he said, 'I can always find you a job here on my fruit farm, you'd get all the fresh air you want.' We learned that his name was David Harrell, and that he grew apples, plums, nuts and soft fruit here in the shelter of the hill.

'How long have you been fruit farming?' I asked him.

'Well, I came to work here when I was about seventeen, a lady called Miss Smith owned the farm at the time. Then later I was called up for National Service and after I came back I started working here again, all the time learning all I could about planting and pruning and marketing. Then in 1975 Miss Smith died, and in 1977 my partner and I bought the fruit farm.'

'How big is it?' I asked.

'We've got 150 acres here, and we grow all sorts of soft fruit as well as about seven or eight different types of apples, and a number of varieties of pears and plums. But we're gradually taking out all the big, tall fruit trees, because it's an uneconomical way of growing them. The modern way is to have short, fairly bushy trees, so that most of the fruit can be picked from a standing position – just a few types need a short step-ladder to reach the tops. That way you get so many more trees to the acre. In the old orchards sixty trees were planted to the acre, but in our new orchards we can plant three hundred. Another

David Harrell in his modern 'Mono' orchard.

thing, with the trees being small it's easy for the tractors and trailers to get up and down the rows.'

I noticed that here and there in between the rows of young apple trees were taller, slimmer bushes, which seemed different to the others.

'What are they doing there?' I asked.

'Ah!' he replied. 'They are most important. This particular area is called a "mono orchard", and is planted entirely with Cox's – a most popular apple – and those odd trees, as you call them, are special. They're a variety of crab apple called *Malus Pollinators*, and they're planted in the orchard to help with pollination. Other crops we grow here are cob nuts, nine acres of them we have.'

'And how do you harvest them?'

'We do that in three stages. Late in September we hand-pick all that we can reach. Then early in October we go along and shake the trees and pick up all the fallen ones. After that we let nature take its course – by the end of October and the beginning of November the rest of the crop simply fall off because they are ripe, so they are all picked up – except the ones that the grey squirrels pinch.'

'And how many people do you employ to keep all these acres going?' I asked.

'My two sons and myself and one other fellow, full-time. But we have quite a few part-time women who work almost all the year round. They help with the pruning, picking and packing, and at the farm shop. What we don't sell locally goes off to the supermarkets, because we belong to the Society of Growers and Traders Marketing Scheme.'

What a marvellous place to live and work – in this lovely, fertile valley, in the shelter of the Cotswold hills. This orchard, David told us, and a couple of others in the area, were planted in 1880 by Lord Sudeley, and he certainly chose a perfect spot for this one.

And so we came at last to Hailes Abbey, or at least what is left of it. All the Cotswold guide books tell in great detail of its history, so I shall not dwell too much on it. It was erected by Richard, Earl of Cornwall, in the thirteenth century, on land that was given to him by his brother, King Henry III. This great Cistercian abbey was really built as a Thanksgiving by Richard, having survived a shipwreck when he was returning from the Holy Land, where he had been on a crusade. Up until the Dissolution of the Monasteries in 1539, pilgrims flocked to the abbey in their thousands, many hoping to see the phial of Holy Blood which Richard's son, Edmund, had presented to the abbey. Years later the contents of the phial were revealed and found to be either honey coloured with saffron or the blood of a duck. It is certainly worth a visit, for it must have been a magnificent place in its day, and there is a wonderful atmosphere there. A sign read 'Hailes Abbey is open to the public, Admission 30p, Senior Citizens 15p.' Beryl turned to me and said with a grin, 'Are you going to own up and go in for 15p?' 'Yes, I think I will today,' I replied, ''cos that man taking the money don't know who I am.' All the same, he gave me a very funny look as I handed him my 15p.

The museum is certainly worth a visit, too, and some of the carved stonework shows the great skill of the masons all those years ago.

Taking a well-earned rest in the ruins of Hailes Abbey.

The little church over the other side of the road, which is nearly a hundred years older than the abbey, is a delight with its many medieval wall paintings and a fifteenth-century rood screen. When we were there a young girl was playing the old organ, which gave the place a marvellous feeling.

But now it was time to retrace our steps, or take the shorter way back which would bring us right outside Mrs Bostock's cottage. We decided on this route, although it would mean that we would not be able to see the tiny church at Farmcote this time. So that was it: along the woodside and right up on the ridge again before dipping down to Wood Stanway. Mrs Bostock was busy chatting to the baker when we passed, so we just said hello and made for the path that would take us to the car.

Greedily we drank coffee from the flask, and ate some home-made cake, very pleased with ourselves, because for the first time we really had not got lost – we had only strayed off the path in Hailes Wood!

Just after this book had been accepted by my publishers I heard that dear, lovable, helpful Mrs Bostock had quite suddenly and unexpectedly died. I felt very sad for days after hearing the news. Whenever I called on her she was cheerful, chatty and smiling. There was always such a welcome too, and yet I had only known her for a short while. What a happier place this would be if there were more Mrs Bostocks in the world!

I like to think of her in heaven, standing just inside the pearly gates, helping St Peter to show folks the way, as she did us and many other travellers. Maybe she's still saying, 'They gets as far as here and they 'ent quite sure whether they should come past here or go up the lane, I tells 'um, you can cut the corner off or go straight on, whichever you do you'll land up in the same place.'

FOUR

Spring in the Cotswolds

Spring had definitely come to the Cotswolds by the time we next walked over the hills and far away – this time from Hailes Abbey to Winchcombe, and then on to Belas Knap.

It was a most beautiful day, with a brilliant blue sky and just a few fluffy clouds here and there. We parked the car outside Hailes church, and set off over the fields to Winchcombe where the marking of the Cotswold Way and signposting were very good. It is a short easy walk to the town along a path called the Pilgrims Way. At one time the track was said to have been paved to make better walking for the pilgrims who came in their thousands to visit Hailes Abbey.

But on this day there were no pilgrims, only Beryl and I and lots of sheep and young lambs, leaping and playing and occasionally losing sight of their mothers, which caused much bleating and baa-ing as one found the other.

The old saying 'It ain't spring till you can plant your foot on twelve daisies at once' was certainly true enough on this day, for the fields were well speckled with them, and we saw our first violets and primroses – 'pimiroses', as my Gramp used to call them. Seeing them reminded me of a little poem by Robert Bridges, which goes:

A-down the meadows green
Let us go dance and play
And look for violets in the lane
And ramble far away
To gather primroses –
That in the woodland grow
And hunt for oxlips, or as yet
The blades of bluebells show.

And indeed we noticed that the bluebells were just thrusting their leaves through to greet the sun – and we saw cowslips too, but only in bud.

The air was filled with the singing of larks, which seemed to be following us along the Cotswold Way. Other birds were busy nest-building, and thrushes and blackbirds and dozens of starlings were shooting about the sky like rockets. Climbing gradually – for here the way was not steep but gently rising – we gazed down into the valley and the town of Winchcombe spread out before us.

The Cotswolds seem to be a very popular place for kissing-gates – well, romantically minded folk call them that – because they are so built that you can trap your sweetheart in them as she, or he, tries to pass through, and then demand a kiss before releasing them. On the other hand, animals can't get through either, so I suppose the gates serve a dual purpose.

After a while we reached a rather muddy lane, and then came on to Puck Pit Lane, which led us to the town.

Mollie at a kissing-gate on the way to Winchcombe.

Winchcombe is a delightful place, sheltered on three sides by the Cotswold hills. We wandered through the streets, where each house, cottage, shop and inn are simply full of character, each different but still in the traditional Cotswold style.

The magnificent wool church, built in 1470, has more gargoyles than any church that I have ever seen, and the most grotesque too! At 'the cross' there is a very interesting museum and outside, under a small slated roof, are the village stocks. Just opposite is the ancient George Inn, which was firstly built as an hostel for wealthy pilgrims visiting Hailes Abbey. In the galleried yard of The George, carved on one of the doors, are the initials of Richard Kydderminster, last but one Abbot of Winchcombe Abbey. Nothing is left of the abbey which was destroyed by Thomas Seymour of Sudeley.

In the sixteenth century, John Stratford of Farmcote started a large-scale tobacco growing industry in Winchcombe which lasted for nearly eighty years. Some of the fine houses in the town were built on the prosperity of the tobacco trade and there is still a road called Tobacco Close and a field called Tobacco Field.

We would have liked to have stayed longer in the town for there is much to see – we hoped to go back later in the day, as I wanted to have a chat with my old friends Mr and Mrs Greening. But first we had to make our way to Belas Knap. Some time ago I had visited this Stone Age burial ground, but then I had travelled out of Winchcombe by car and walked across two or three fields to get to it. But this time, we were *walking* the Cotswold Way, and the map told us that we had to leave the A46 a little way away from Sudeley Castle. Soon we spotted a sign which told us that Belas Knap was, in fact, 2¼ kms away. And what a climb it was! Up and up we walked, often stopping, both to get our breath and to admire the view of Winchcombe and Sudeley Castle. (The castle is rich in Tudor history. Catherine Parr, last of Henry's wives, lived there after marrying Baron Seymour of Sudeley, and is buried there. The castle is often open to the public, a treat not to be missed.) Along the way we saw more blue violets and primroses and bright yellow blossoms on the gorse bushes. There's an old saying that 'Kissing's out of fashion when the gorse is not in bloom'. Well, you can always find a few flowers blooming, no matter what the weather, and kissing's never out of fashion. In the hedges the wild cherry and blackthorn blossoms were past their best but the 'bread and cheese' – what we as children used to call the young leaves of the may bushes – were just beginning to show.

This must have been one of the hardest climbs so far – the going was so steep that we were both puffing and blowing like a couple of broken-winded teapots. Halfway up we reached Wadfield Farm. Apparently the name derives from a field called Woadfield, where woad plants were once specially grown, the roots of which were used for dyeing wool. On and on we went, climbing all the time until we reached Humblebee Wood – and then, suddenly there it was, Belas Knap, looking like a great green stranded whale on the skyline. No wonder we were puffed, for now we were 900 feet up.

Belas Knap is a long barrow burial chamber of the Stone Age people. My old friend, Mr Greening, had told me much about this place, for he had come up here as an interested spectator when Sir James Berry, the famous surgeon and a Fellow of the Society of Antiquarians was excavating Belas Knap between 1928 and 1930 when quite a lot of flints and bones were found. The burial chamber had first been opened by the Dents of Sudeley in 1863, when vandals broke in and smashed up some of the skeletons. At another time, during excavations, a nightwatchman, a Mr Aston, was hired to keep an eye on the place. Late one night some of the local lads played a trick on him. One fellow with a sheet flung over his head pretended to be a ghost from the burial chamber, hid behind a stone wall and called out in an eerie voice 'Aston, Aston, why troublest thou me?' Poor old Aston was scared out of his wits and leaped to his feet, and ran for all he was worth through the long grass and down Humblebee Wood. The story goes that where old Aston scuffed his feet through the grass, none has ever grown since.

But on the day we were up there all was quiet and peaceful. We walked around the huge stone-built barrow, and marvelled at the wonderful dry stone-walling which dates from between 4000 and 5000 BC, an art which is still carried on in exactly the same way.

The name Belas Knap is derived from 'bel' which in olden times meant a 'beacon' and 'cnaepp' which meant a hilltop.

At this point we decided to walk on to Wontley Farm – this would save us walking up all this way again to do the next little bit of the walk. So off we went as far as Wontley, and then turned back and round to Belas Knap again. We took the shorter way down, through the fields and onto the road – all downhill, thank goodness! – which took us right into Winchcombe and then onto Gretton Road and my old friends, the Greenings, who were waiting for us with welcome cups of tea and delicious home-made scones and jam. After we had regaled ourselves with the lovely tea that Mrs Greening had prepared for us, I talked to Mr Greening, and asked him to tell me a little bit about life as it was in Winchcombe years ago.

'I was born in a cottage on Gretton Road in Winchcombe in 1903, and have lived there and nearby all my life. I come from an ancestry stretching back many generations who also lived hereabouts. In my teenage years I realised that I was witnessing the tail-end of the premechanical age, for the internal combustion engine had arrived, and with great rapidity the older ways were being eroded, so that life in our market town was gradually changing – changing a way of life as it had been for centuries.

'When we were young, all the children up the northern end of the town played for hours at the crossroads, but when the old lamplighter came along at dusk and lit the gas street-lamp, I knew then that it was time to go home – so home I went as I knew if I delayed it, there would be a good clout from my father. Of course, years ago there were toll gates at each entry point into Winchcombe, and there were two pounds, where any animals that were found straying were shut in, and before the owners of the straying animals could claim their sheep or cattle, a fine had to be paid. My grandfather worked in the tanyard, where animal skins were treated to produce very fine leather. He was the foreman there and it was his job to ring the 'Tanyard bell' to let the workers know when it was time to stop and start work. My grandfather gave the bell to me, and in turn I gave it to our museum in Winchcombe: I thought that it was the right place for it.

'In my boyhood days there was a little cottage shop kept by Mrs Mary Yiend. She sold cakes, sweets and treacle and we always called her "Treacle Mary". Besides selling sweets she made and sold rice puddings – in great earthenware dishes she cooked them, cutting it out cold in lumps in ha'porths and penn'orths. She would say when we went in to buy a piece, "Will you have it in your hand or in some paper?" But before you could reply she'd taken your money and slapped the cold pudding in your hand.

'Many years ago, some of the pubs used to give their customers a bite to eat on Christmas Day. Apparently one Christmas a regular fellow to one of the pubs was a bit late coming in for his Christmas eats, so the landlady said to him, "I spose thee bist come for thee bit of victuals?"

'"Yes please ma'am," he replied.

'"Well thee cosn't a'none 'cos 'tis all yut," she told him.

'One fellow who lived hereabout,' Mr Greening went on, 'was a bit on the lazy side, anyhow his wife was expecting her first child anytime. She woke up in the night and she knew that it wouldn't be long before the baby was born, as she had terrible pains.

'"Jack," she cried, "quick, quick, go and fetch the midwife."

'Jack just turned over in his sleep and mumbled, "Cosn't thee put it off till morning, woman?"

'Yes, life has certainly changed here over the years, gone are the old horse buses that took people in to Cheltenham to do a bit of shopping, and the funeral hearses that could be hired along with four black horses. Many of the old inns and cider mills have disappeared, too, and I am glad that I was privileged enough to remember the old ways, the old days. How true are these lines that were written by Wordsworth:

> It is not now as it has been of yore
> The things which I have seen, I now can see no more.

I turned to Marion Greening, and asked her to tell me a little of her life in Winchcombe.

'Well, I was born in Winchcombe and have lived here all my life. I left school at fourteen, in 1921, and the very next day started work in a local emporium. Our hours were from 9 a.m. till 7 p.m., Mondays, Tuesdays and Wednesdays. Early closing was on each Thursday. Fridays it was 9 a.m. till 8 p.m. and Saturdays 9 a.m. till 9 p.m., with an hour for dinner, of course. My wages were three shillings a week for fifty-seven hours, with a two-shilling rise every two years, so that by the time I left to be married I was getting eleven shillings a week.

'We assistants were expected to serve in all the departments, whether it be anything and everything in the drapery line, haberdashery, household goods, boots and shoes, men's and boys' clothes, lino, mats and carpets. One of my first jobs was to sweep out the shop on Mondays and Thursdays. Everything had to be covered with dust sheets the night before. I had to sprinkle water lightly over the wooden floors with an old watering can, to help lay the dust before sweeping.

'My next job on fine days was to do what was known as "dressing out". This meant displaying goods outside the shop, on the path. On wooden boards stood on a couple of empty boxes, I placed unbleached sheeting, calico, casements and cretonnes, shoes, boots, slippers, men's and boys' clothing, and coconut matting – anything to tempt the customers inside.

'Each February, one window was always dressed as a "black window", with everything that was needed for a bereavement, even to black-edged handkerchiefs and black hair-ribbon. In those days, even children were dressed in black or grey when a member of the family died.

'Of course, if anyone of any consequence died in the town, a black painted board was fixed down the centre of the shop windows as a mark of respect.

'After I'd been there for some time, our milliner left and, as I was handy with my needle, I was asked to make hats, trimming them with lots of artificial flowers, cherries and feathers. I did alterations, too, to clothes that were bought there. Another job I did was to make about two hundred rosettes each year for the Agricultural Show. One year I asked if I could have an hour off to go to the Show to see all those lovely rosettes I'd made presented. "No," I was told firmly, "your place is in the shop." Of course, there was never a moment's rest, for there were always price tags to be sewn on, sewing socks, stockings and gloves together in pairs, and a hundred and one other jobs waiting to be done.

'At Christmas our millinery room was made into a toy bazaar, which of course brought in a lot of customers. I think on those few evenings before Christmas it must have been near midnight before I got home. In those days we didn't need youth clubs and discos to use up our surplus energy. The only thing we needed to do when we got home was to have something to eat, and crawl into bed. For we would have been on our feet all day, we were never allowed to sit down, at all. In wintertime the shop was very cold with only a small coke-burning stove, but at least it had a long flue pipe on, and when no one was looking we'd warm our hands on it.

'I worked there for seven years before leaving to get married. Just after we returned from our honeymoon, the wife of the owner of the emporium called with a wedding present, and asked if I would go back and work part-time. "Certainly not," my husband shouted to her.

'After she had gone, I unwrapped the wedding present. It was a toast rack, EPNS, with the price tag marked 3/9 on it. It still hangs up in the shed covered in verdigris, the price tag long since rotted off. I leave it there to remind me of seven years that I wouldn't like to relive again. Of course times have changed very much since then, especially living and working conditions, which is a good thing.

'Over the years I've always taken a great interest in the town – I belonged to Winchcombe WI for years and joined the local art and flower arranging classes. And although I'm partially disabled I still enjoy my painting classes, but can't manage to compete in the floral exhibitions any more.'

Of course, both Mr and Mrs Greening were a mine of information about Winchcombe, but time was pressing, and we had to get back to Hailes church and the car. Bless his heart, Mr Greening announced that he would drive us there in his lovely vintage 1950 MG. Purred along, it did, with no effort at all! We hadn't gone far when Mr

Greening said, 'If you have got half an hour to spare I would like you to meet Doctor de Vere Short. He has retired now, but he was the family doctor here for many years, a much loved and highly respected man, and a very good friend of ours.'

After a little while Mr Greening pulled up at a lovely Cotswold stone house and we went in to meet Doctor Short, a charming man who told me that he trained at Trinity College, Dublin. 'I qualified in 1932 and took my first post as house surgeon at Preston Royal Infirmary,' he told us. 'Then over the years I had a very varied career in different hospitals and towns. After the war we settled in Winchcombe. At that time there was only a small hospital here, it only dealt with general surgery and medical care, with no maternity unit at all. So most women had their babies at home – unless there were complications, then they had to be taken to Cheltenham Hospital.

'Once,' he went on, 'I was called out to a farm up on the hills' – I realised that when the doctor spoke of 'up on the hills', it could be any one of the remote villages or lonely farms that were part of his huge practice – 'I reached the farm where the farmer's wife was in labour, the nurse was already there, and everything was going fine. Well, after a while the baby was born and mother and child settled down for the night, so I thought I'd leave for home. When I got to the bottom of the stairs the farmer was sitting there with a shotgun under his arm. "Going shooting?" I asked. "No, not now," he replied, "but if anything had gone wrong that would have been one shot for you and one for the nurse."

'Another time I was called out late at night. The woman was frantic – one of her twin daughters was very ill and could I come at once. When I got there the child looked terrible – she had breathing difficulties, mouth open, eyes rolling. I suspected meningitis and soon had the child in an ambulance and into Cheltenham Hospital where doctors started to treat the youngster at once. There was nothing more I could do so I left for home. I hadn't been there long when there was another frantic call from the mother to say that the other twin had the same symptoms. Sure enough, when I got there I could see that the child was desperately ill, but I thought it very unlikely that both could have

Mollie with Mr and Mrs Greening.

meningitis. Then I asked the mother, "Where have the children been today?" "Out in the fields with me, we've been potato-picking. They came but played in the hedge while I worked."

'That was it, belladonna poisoning, deadly nightshade: the children had eaten some of the berries. Another dash to the hospital with the second child, where they were both soon treated – thankfully, for only mild poisoning – and, of course, they both recovered.

'I have had a wonderful time living and working here at Winchcombe, especially with all the marvellous advancements in medical treatment. I've mixed in with the community here, played cricket, joined the local drama group, and made many, many friends. I'm so glad I chose to settle in Winchcombe.'

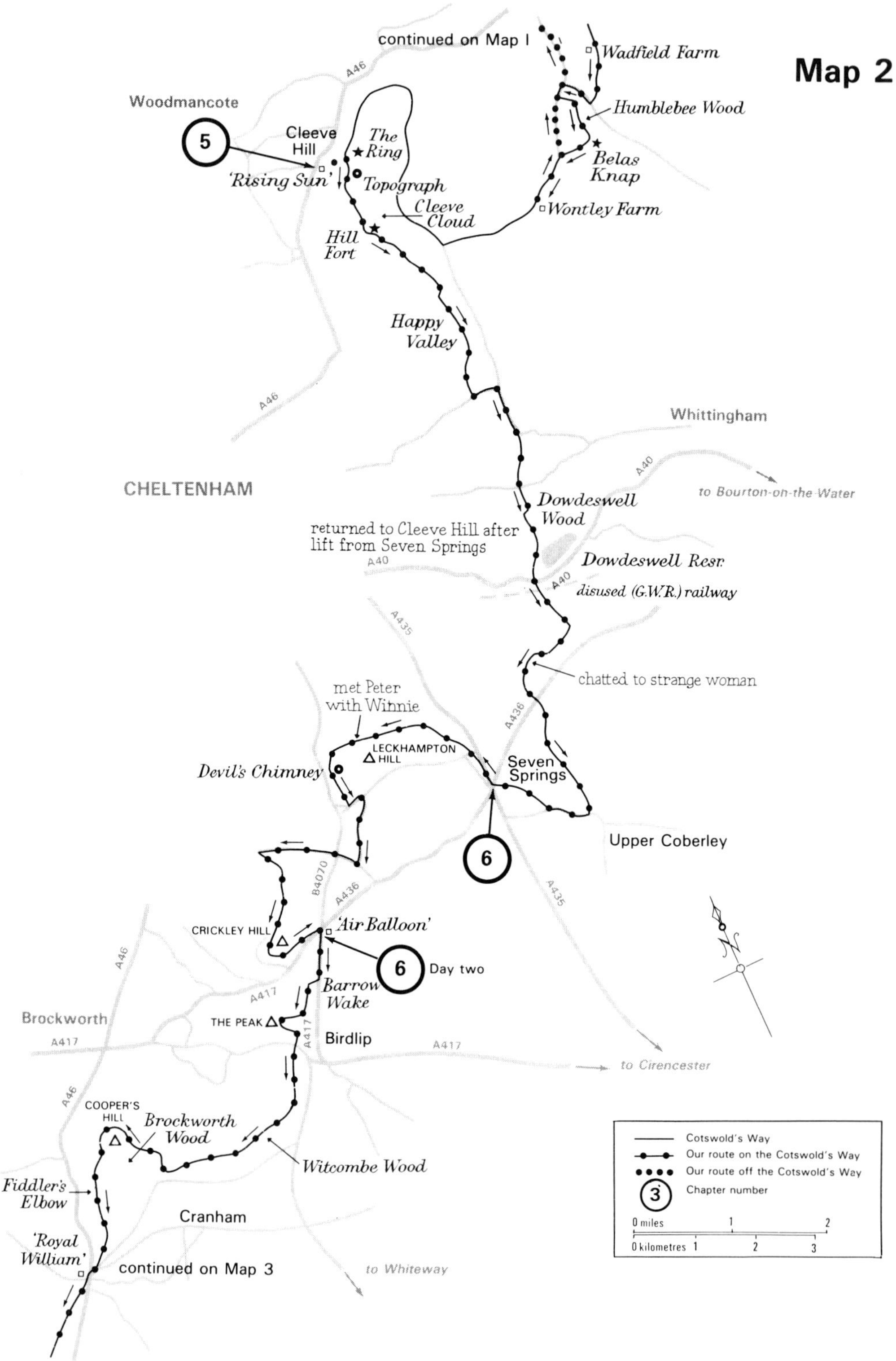
Map 2
continued on Map I
Wadfield Farm
Humblebee Wood
Woodmancote
A46
5
Cleeve Hill
The Ring
'Rising Sun'
Topograph
Belas Knap
Wontley Farm
Cleeve Cloud
Hill Fort
Happy Valley
A46
Whittingham
A40
CHELTENHAM
to Bourton-on-the-Water
Dowdeswell Wood
returned to Cleeve Hill after lift from Seven Springs
A40
Dowdeswell Resr.
A40
disused (G.W.R.) railway
A435
chatted to strange woman
met Peter with Winnie
A436
LECKHAMPTON HILL
Devil's Chimney
Seven Springs
6
Upper Coberley
B4070
A436
A435
CRICKLEY HILL
'Air Balloon'
A46
6
Day two
Barrow Wake
A417
Brockworth
THE PEAK
A417
Birdlip
A417
A417
to Cirencester
A46
COOPER'S HILL
Brockworth Wood
Witcombe Wood
Fiddler's Elbow
Cranham
'Royal William'
continued on Map 3
to Whiteway
Cotswold's Way
Our route on the Cotswold's Way
Our route off the Cotswold's Way
3
Chapter number
0 miles 1 2
0 kilometres 1 2 3

FIVE

Where Larks Fly High

Had we gone back to Wontley Farm at the start of the next walk, we would have walked almost in a circle. So, to save doubling back on ourselves, we took advice from one of the Cotswold Way books and made our way straight to the A46, which is the Winchcombe–Cheltenham road. A few miles along there we came to an inn called The Rising Sun; from here, after parking the car, we walked straight to Cleeve Hill, from which we were to walk to Seven Springs – our planned route for the day.

The way up to the great green plateau of Cleeve was very steep. There were several different paths leading to the top, for it is a favourite place for walkers, with or without dogs, and for youngsters riding horses as well.

The day was clear and bright and still a bit breezy. When we reached the top ridge, we were almost at the highest point on the Cotswold Way – 1000 feet up. There surely is a spirit in these hills that puts a buoyancy in our step, and we don't get half so winded as we did at first. Now we seem to almost glide over the changing wolds, where every hilltop and every valley presents a wonderful picture that no artist could paint or capture. Of course the *very* steep walks still make us puff and blow a bit, but the further along the Cotswold Way we travel the more enjoyable it becomes.

We were still climbing, and by now we were 1085 feet up – truly the highest point on the Cotswold Way. Once again the views were indescribably wonderful – Bredon Hill looked so very close you felt you could almost reach out and touch it, and the Malvern Hills, a bit further over, were etched out very clearly, too. Away on the horizon we could just make out the smudgy outline of the Welsh mountains. The town of Cheltenham was spread out below us, and the larks were singing as they flew up and up into the brilliant blue sky. So many poets, like Margaret Rhodes, have described larks high over the

Cotswold hills, 'singing their hearts out while the sky trembles with their song'.

Before we made our way over the hills to Dowdeswell reservoir, I went to meet an eighty-year-old retired farmer, Mr Victor Haslum, who lives at Dryfield Farm on the other side of Cleeve Hill, 700 feet up on the Cotswolds.

I asked Mr Haslum how long he had been farming on Cleeve.

'All my life,' he said, 'my father was a farmer here too and so were both my brothers. See that farm down there in the valley? That's where we all lived before coming up here to Dryfield Farm.

'I worked with horses almost all my farming life,' he went on, 'at one time we had nine working horses on this farm. We used to go to Wales to buy most of them – of course they were not broken in to do farm work, and to get them used to us we fed them on dry grub, that way they began to get a bit friendly. It used to take us about six months to break them in properly. In my latter years I did use tractors for some things, but I still kept horses for the bulk of the work and I bred a few shire horses too.'

We went into the farmhouse. On the wall hung a lovely photo of two beautiful grey cart-horses ploughing, with Mr Haslum walking behind driving them. I asked him if they were special.

'All our horses were special,' he replied, 'but those were the last two I had so they were extra special – Captain and Prince they were called – most beautiful animals they were and they understood every word I said to them.'

'How many acres did you farm up here?'

'About five hundred,' he replied.

From the farmhouse window I could see that the hills and valleys beyond were speckled with hundreds of sheep.

'Did you keep sheep?' I enquired.

'Oh, yes, hundreds of 'em, well, five hundred-odd at most times. Wonderful animals for the land, sheep are.' He went on, 'You see they eat the grass down very short, which helps to make it grow thick again, and then there's the manure. Oh yes, sheep do the ground a powerful lot of good. Some weeks we would send fifty or sixty good

The hills were speckled with sheep (*photograph by Stan Partlett*).

fat sheep to Birmingham for selling in the butchers' shops. We had to drive them along the road from here at Dryfield to Winchcombe railway station, a matter of about four miles. 'Course, we always had a couple of good working sheepdogs to help keep the flock in order. We had to take them steady and not get them on the run. They were quite fat, you see, and only used to leisurely roaming over the Cotswold hills. Father always followed behind with a horse and float in case any of the animals conked out. If this happened, they would be lifted up into the float for the rest of the journey. After a bit of a rest the sheep got their wind back, and joined the rest of the flock when we loaded them into a railway truck. We grew a good few acres of roots – swedes and turnips – to feed them on in the wintertime when there wasn't much grass about.

'We had a herd of cows, too, and beside that we had a milk round and delivered milk to the houses on Cleeve Hill and to many of the villages around. When the weather was bad – and we do get it a bit fierce up here come winter – I know the time when I've had to carry two two-gallon pails of milk on a wooden yoke on my shoulders and walk for miles and miles to get the milk to some of the folk who lived in the outlying places, and sometimes never got home for my dinner till half-past two. And one day, when I got back late, I was that hungry and thirsty I felt "atto in the middle",* so I went straight into the barn where we kept our home-made cider. On the shelf was a few special bottles, put aside for somebody no doubt. I took hold of the cider mug that was kept in there so that any of us could have a drink, and filled it up with some of that special cider. I had one mugful before going indoors for my dinner. I ate it all right, but didn't half feel bad – I suppose it was drinking on an empty stomach. Anyhow, I had to rush outside and was I sick as a dog in the pig tub where all the vegetable peelings and swill was emptied and later fed to the pigs!

'In the winter of 1947 I was the only person able to get out on to the by-road up here for six weeks with horse and cart, the snow was so bad: the snow was as high as old Punch the horse, and he plunged his way through it. There's no other word for it. As fast as the council

* 'in two in the middle' – hungry.

Mr Victor Haslam: a lifetime with horses (*photographs kindly supplied by the late Victor Haslam*).

dug a track on the road, it filled up with snow again. I was the only person to tackle the main road for days and days. And the frost was so severe that I had to break the ice in Langley Brook twice a day with a stone hammer so that the animals could get a drink.

'We used to show some of the cattle at the agricultural shows around Gloucester, Cheltenham and Winchcombe, and over the years we had several prizes for our Hereford bulls, and our sheep and horses. We used to take the horses down into Winchcombe to be shod; there were three blacksmiths and two farriers working there at one time.

'When we were all working out in the harvest fields, our mother used to bring our tea out to us in a great big wicker basket. There was plenty of tea, bacon sandwiches and home-made cake for the four of us. And of course we boys used to shoot at the rabbits as they rushed out of the corn as the binder came round. On this particular day we had shucked up half the field with sheaves of corn, when I saw a rabbit rush in to what he thought would be a safe place. I took a pot shot at him, not realising the basket of tea things was in there. There was such a noise as my shots landed, and cups, food, tea can and bits of basket flew up in the air – and the rabbit rushed out unscathed to live, at least, for another day.

'Of course I still live here at Dryfield, but these days I leave the farming to someone else.'

After saying goodbye to Mr Haslum, we then had to make our way over to the other side of Cleeve Hill to get back on to the Cotswold Way.

The walk from then on – until we got almost to the Dowdeswell reservoir – was quite uneventful. We passed over some roughish ground and an area called Happy Valley, and saw a number of gorse bushes in bloom, and the bluebells and cowslips were out in great profusion with plenty of stitchwort on the hedge banks, and the beautiful pale fresh green leaves on the trees – that lovely green that only lasts a few weeks. It really was a lovely time of the year, with cuckoos calling all over the hills, and all around the sheep-spangled slopes that are so typical of the Cotswolds.

After walking for about an hour, we reached Dowdeswell Wood, and with the day being quite warm we were glad of the shade that it offered us. But quite suddenly it seemed a bit creepy – an almost clammy cold in there – and we learned later that that particular part of the wood is supposed to be haunted by the ghost of a man who was hanged thereabouts for stealing a sheep. At last we reached the busy A40: this we had to cross and watch out for a sign that would point the way to Seven Springs and Leckhampton Hill. We crossed over what was once the old GWR railway line – the track had been long since removed. On and on we went looking for white spots, leaving a small wood on our left. Although we had our field maps and the little green Cotswold Way book, we still seemed to go off the track a bit. One minute, we were just chatting and going ahead, but the next we found that we were once more slightly lost. We saw what we thought was a white spot, but on closer inspection found that it was nothing but bird lime. It was time to stop and get out the map and find our bearings once again.

After a while, we came to a very steep hill with wooden steps – to make it a bit easier for the walker, I suppose. It was quite the steepest hill that we had yet climbed. There were trees on both sides with a few flowers here and there – pink campions, foxgloves and honeysuckle winding round the bushes. We reached the top and gladly threw ourselves down on the cool grass to rest and get our breath back. The grass was close-cropped as if rabbits fed there, and there were quite a few small wild flowers growing – yellow babies'-rattles, silverweed and daisies.

As we lay there, full-length, gazing up at the perfect blue sky, suddenly a strange woman came out of the bushes: she saw us, and with the look of a trapped animal, she turned quickly and started to go back from where she had come.

'Please don't be afraid,' I called, quite gently. 'We shan't hurt you.'

She paused for a moment and then she came back and stood for a minute eyeing us up and down.

'Why don't you sit down with us and have a rest?' Beryl said.

The woman looked at us suspiciously.

'It's all right, we're just out walking like you.'

Having decided that we were quite harmless, the woman – who was about sixty odd, I would think – squatted down on her haunches, a little way away from us. She had a fine clear skin and eyes, and was as weatherbeaten as a gypsy. Immediately I remembered a poem we learned at school, 'Old Meg she was a gypsy and lived upon the moor', but here was no gypsy. This woman spoke in quite a cultured voice, yet with a country dialect. She had an old brown felt hat on, a fawn raincoat and what looked like men's boots. She caught my glance.

'I used to have proper walking boots like you,' she said, 'but they wore out.'

We shared our boiled sweets with her, telling her where we planned to walk to over the summer months. Then gradually, she started telling us about herself.

'I expect you wonder who I am, and what I'm doing in this wood. Well, it's a long story,' she went on. 'I was only nineteen when the last war broke out, and my young man, Andrew, and I were very much in love and had planned to marry the next year. He was a few years older than I, and was soon called up into the RAF. He trained as a pilot, and within a few months he was shot down during the Battle of Britain, over the sea somewhere.'

She paused for a moment, with a faraway look in her eyes, as if she were going all through those sad days again. Beryl and I remained silent. The woman went on.

'I just never got over it, so I took to the roads, tramping all over Great Britain. I used to earn money fruit- and pea-picking, and potato-picking in the autumn. I saved quite a bit of money that way: my needs were very few. Then one day I found this wood, and decided that this was where I was going to "pitch my tent" – not that I'd got a tent – but I did make myself a sort of hut. I found a lot of discarded wood. Oh, yes, quite dry and comfortable it was. I lived on herbs and berries and birds' eggs, but I used to walk into the town to get sugar, tea, flour and a bit of fat, and sometimes I'd buy some meat – but not very often. That was how the local authorities found out about me. One day I was followed, and they said it wasn't a fit place to live, and carted me off to a hostel. I hated it there and ran away. I went back to my wood – but they always found me. Finally, I was given a council bungalow and, providing I kept it clean and did the garden and didn't go off again, they agreed to pay my rent and rates and I get enough social security to live on. But on days like this I just shut the door and come out in these woods, going back late in the evening. Oh, it's a fair walk to my bungalow, but I don't mind. A day out here in God's good air and with all the wonderful things there are to see, does me the world of good, and I shall keep coming here for as long as I can.'

Then quite suddenly she got up to leave. She picked up her stick and an old hessian bag that was half full of something or other and turned back into the wood, calling goodbye as she went. We called back goodbye, but she was most likely out of earshot by then.

Beryl and I just looked at each other in amazement – not really believing that it had happened. Time we got on our way, anyhow.

From then on it was easy going down through a wooded area, and soon we reached the roadway. Neither of us liked road walking after the grass tracks we had got used to, and apparently there was an alternative route via Upper Coberley, but I did want to paddle at Seven Springs – reputed to be the source of the River Thames – and having passed the spot many times in the car we now wanted to have a good look at it.

There was quite a nice little trickle coming from somewhere in the rocks and greenery, so we caught some in our hands and had a drink of the cool spring water, and I had a paddle.

We still had to get back to where we had parked the car, but first we thought we would have a rest and a little light refreshment from our back packs. As we had made quite good time, we decided that we would walk back the way we had come. Some people sitting near us heard what we were planning and offered to give us a lift. They dropped us on the A40 as they were on their way back to Oxford, and we set off over the hills again to Cleeve, and finally to where the car was parked.

We really must have walked about ten or twelve miles on that day, but what a super one!

SIX

Summertime and the Fields Are All Buttercuppy

On each of the next two days of our walk we covered an awful lot of ground. This was because my son, Peter, was on holiday. Each day he would drive us to the starting point, meet us halfway with some refreshment, and leave Beryl and I to walk another five or six miles. At the end of the day he would be cheerfully waiting for us. In fact, we covered as much ground in two days as we would have normally walked in six.

The first day he was with us he drove us to Seven Springs, which was as far as we had got on our last walk, and dropped us there. Then he went on in the car to Leckhampton, where he would park the car and walk up to meet us with Winnie, the boxer. So, with that all fixed up Beryl and I set off at a goodly pace along the road part of the Cotswold Way before turning up a path which led into a lane that took us up rather a steep hill on to Charlton Kings Common, where there were lots of gorse bushes and scrub. On the top of the hill we turned and looked back to Cleeve Common and beyond to Cheltenham, hardly believing that we had walked all the way from Cleeve Hill to where we were now standing. We went on through some old stone quarries, and on to Leckhampton Hill with the Devil's Chimney just away to our left. This high stone column is said to have been left by the quarrymen who for many years dug stones from the deep quarry there. Now the common is filled with bushes and trees, and is a haven for all sorts of birds, and there were bumblebees, butterflies and buttercups everywhere.

From up front somewhere we could hear the joyous sound of Winnie barking with delight at something or other, and then suddenly round the bend they came – so pleased to see us, they were. We sat as near to the Devil's Chimney as we could safely get. Peter had brought coffee and sandwiches up with him so we all had a wonderful picnic – gazing out onto the city of Gloucester miles away. After a good rest

Mollie with Winnie the boxer near the Devil's Chimney.

we all set off to walk down the hill towards the car.

Beryl and I were not the least bit tired, so while Peter drove off to The Air Balloon pub car park a few miles away – where he would wait for us – we set off over the hills again towards Crickley Hill, where folk have lived since the Stone Age. We met lots of people walking – because Crickley Hill is a country park, this is a favourite spot for families to walk and picnic in. It is also very hilly and a famous archaeological site dating back to 2500 BC – during the summer months organised 'digs' are carried out, and there is a photographic exhibition of tools and bracelets and other objects. Again the views are spectacular – we could see for miles and miles. Apart from going through a rather lovely wood, the walk turned out to be very straightforward, with no villages along the way, so it didn't take us long to get to The Air Balloon pub. Although it was quite early in the afternoon, we did think that we had done extremely well that day and sank gratefully into the car. I for one was thankful that at least someone else was going to drive home.

'Can you see the Black Mountains?' (*photograph by E. Buckland*).

Next day was another lovely summer morning, so we left home quite early, eager to be off again over the hills. Peter again drove us to our starting point. He parked once more at The Air Balloon, and he and Winnie walked with us for a while, up as far as Barrow Wake. We went right to the peak, 800–900 feet up. Nearby there is a stone memorial to a geologist named Peter Hopkins, and a topograph marked with pointers to May Hill and the Malverns and other high spots to look for. From there we could see the outline of the Black Mountains and the Brecon Beacons, and the air was like wine.

Once again there were lots of people walking over the hills, not just keeping to the Cotswold Way, but all over the fields. We could see several cars parked over to our left in a lay-by, which many folk call Birdlip. From the lay-by you can get stupendous views of Gloucester and beyond. Peter turned to go back, with the promise to meet us in Birdlip village.

These long stretches of uplands were once the old sheep walks, and remnants of a way of travel long since forgotten. Here and there in the close-cropped grass small blue harebells were growing – the colour of the summer sky they were – and masses of fragrant pink thyme, which is what gives the mutton such a wonderful flavour. It was so plentiful that I picked some, and stuffed it in my back pack. I would take it home and dry it, and use it in wintertime stuffings.

In no time at all, it seemed, we reached Birdlip village. A chat to Peter and a drink from the flask, and then I set out to find Mr Ted Partridge, a Cotswold builder, with whom I wanted to have a chat about his work in this area. But Mr Partridge said no, he didn't like to do that sort of thing.

So I thanked him and went back to find Peter, Beryl and Winnie.

While I had gone, Peter, Beryl and Winnie had had a nice long rest. But the day was quite young, and I for one was not ready to go home. Beryl, too, was quite keen, so we set off and arranged to meet Peter at a point near Cranham Corner.

We set off through the beautiful Witcombe Woods. Here the trees were mostly beech. Very tall they were, as if they were sending their branches up to the light, with thick roots clinging on to the banksides. We were glad of the welcome shade the trees offered us for the day was rather hot, as it had only just turned midday. At that moment, surely, summer was at its peak. Here, too, there was an abundance of wild flowers, red and white campion, St John's wort, pyramid orchids, wild pansies and masses of Tom Thumbs and babies' rattles, and all along the pathway on both sides were bright red wild strawberries. I hadn't tasted wild strawberries since I was a child, when we used to walk up to Gorsehill Woods about three miles from our cottage in Ducklington, just to pick and eat this delicious fruit. We picked handfuls of Witcombe strawberries, quenching our thirst with their summer sweetness.

Thankfully it was downhill most of the way and as cool as a church in that thickly wooded glade. There was an unmistakable smell of summer blossoms coupled with the lush green growth of the wood, and it was all very wonderful. According to our map there are the remains of a Roman villa in these woods, but it is not, at present, open to the public. Such quietness, apart from birdsong, was unbelievable.

We had promised to meet Peter alongside the wood, just beyond Cooper's Hill. This meant that we should have to walk up the hill, and coming at the end of quite a strenuous day we found the going extremely hard. Had we not promised to meet Peter, we would have missed walking up Cooper's Hill and gone around by a place called Fiddler's Elbow, still hilly but not too bad.

Anyhow, the hill had to be tackled. One guide book describes it as 'perpendicular, climbing not advised'. We began by walking through a section of hilly, winding woodland, and suddenly there it was – this great steep hill! We struggled up it – that's the only word for it. I stopped and rested several times for a puff and a blow, and Beryl – who is years younger than me – also had to stop for breath three or four times. It is here, at Cooper's Hill, that people have gathered for centuries in the springtime, for the cheese-rolling ceremony down this one-in-one slope. The contestants, hundreds of them, apparently chase several seven-pound Gloucester cheeses down the hill, and whoever catches a cheese keeps it as a reward. Looking at the sheer sides of the hill I would think that there must be a few contestants rolling down along with the cheeses, too. The ceremony is now held on the Spring Bank Holiday.

We eventually reached the top of the hill where we found a maypole or flag-staff with a cockerel on top of it. From then on we just followed our noses through quite a thick wood, known as Brockworth. There were several paths but we kept to the one that was the most worn. After walking for about fifteen minutes we reached the roadway, and came out exactly where we'd planned, at Cranham Corner, and at once saw the blue Metro parked in the shade about fifty yards along the road – but no Peter! I had the spare car keys with me, and we thankfully sat in the car for a few minutes to recover. Once again, we heard Winnie barking, and soon both Peter and the dog came into sight a little way along the road. He had taken one of the paths in Brockworth Wood and we another, but it was only a matter of a few minutes between our emerging at one place and his at another.

After another lovely day, it was time to make our way home.

SEVEN

A Day for Dawdling

Today we began our walk where we ended last time – near Cranham Corner. Our target today was Painswick, which is only a matter of two and a half miles from there. After seeking permission, we parked the car in the Royal William Inn car park, then made our way up a narrow road alongside it. We walked for about a quarter of a mile, travelling slightly uphill all the while – according to the map this would eventually take us up on to Painswick Beacon and the golf course there. Even there the walker still has the right of way, and the Cotswold white spot is much in evidence.

And what a wonderful walk it was. We strode along in bright sunshine, under a clear blue sky, enjoying the gently bracing air and the beautiful views which could be seen to our left between the wooded hillsides. Somewhere near here is a little hamlet called Paradise. The name is said to have been given to it by Charles II when he visited the area, and no wonder – this walk is truly a magical paradise. The valley runs steeply down, again to our left, and then rises up again just as steeply, so that we were on a level with another hillside a few miles away, where the villages of Sheepscombe, Slad and Bulls Cross lay bathing in the summer sunshine. It was a day for dawdling, and we were taking it very slowly. We should have to walk back to the car, of course, but even then it wouldn't be as long a walk as usual.

Along this part of the Cotswold Way are hundreds of pine trees and masses of wild flowers everywhere – foxgloves, dog roses, elderflowers, honeysuckle, rosebay willowherb and lots of orchids. On the close-cropped grass the tiny blue harebell and great patches of wild thyme were still blooming. We sat and rested for a while, lying in the hot sun on clumps of thyme – its delicate perfume was with us all day long. We reached an old stone quarry called Catsbrain, and then walked on through another stretch of woodland before reaching the roadway, which took us through Painswick. Situated between two

Map 3

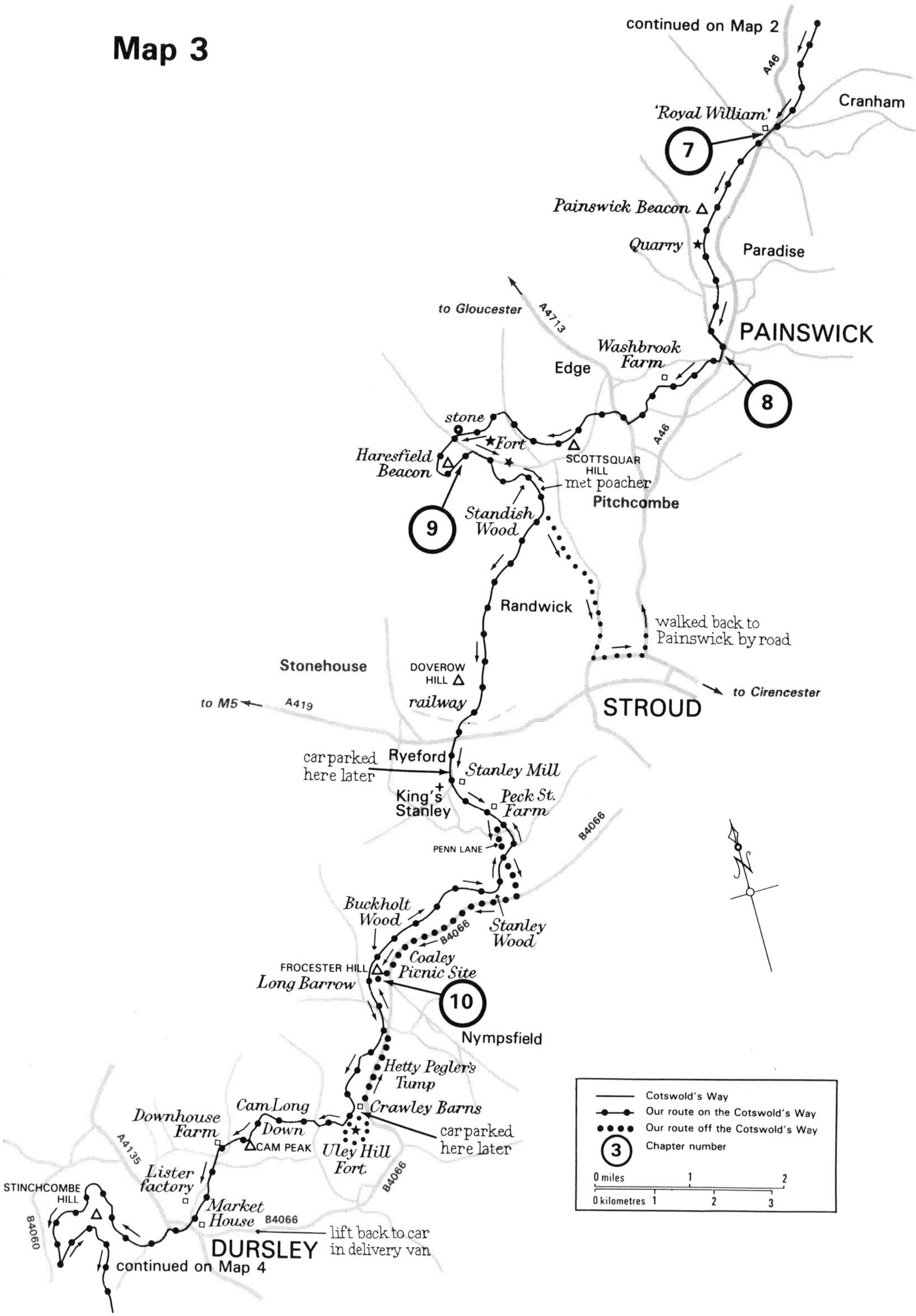

continued on Map 2
A46
Cranham
'Royal William'
7
Painswick Beacon
Quarry
Paradise
to Gloucester
A4173
PAINSWICK
Washbrook Farm
Edge
8
stone
Fort
A46
Haresfield Beacon
SCOTTSQUAR HILL
met poacher
Pitchcombe
9
Standish Wood
Randwick
walked back to Painswick by road
Stonehouse
DOVEROW HILL
to M5
A419
railway
STROUD
to Cirencester
car parked here later
Ryeford
Stanley Mill
King's Stanley
Peck St. Farm
B4066
PENN LANE
Buckholt Wood
B4066
Stanley Wood
Coaley Picnic Site
FROCESTER HILL
Long Barrow
10
Nympsfield
Hetty Pegler's Tump
Crawley Barns
Cam Long Down
Downhouse Farm
CAM PEAK
Uley Hill Fort
car parked here later
A4135
Lister factory
B4066
STINCHCOMBE HILL
Market House
B4066
B4060
DURSLEY
lift back to car in delivery van
continued on Map 4
Cotswold's Way
Our route on the Cotswold's Way
Our route off the Cotswold's Way
3 Chapter number
0 miles 1 2
0 kilometres 1 2 3

A busy street in Painswick.

valleys, the town is delightful – no wonder one writer described it as 'the Jewel of the Cotswolds'. All the buildings, shops, inns, picturesque weavers' cottages and large private houses – mostly built by the cloth mill owners – are a joy to see. Many of them date from the fifteenth, sixteenth and seventeenth centuries, when the wool trade was flourishing here – the post office is an outstanding fifteenth-century timber framed building, which is much photographed. The church is very beautiful and worth a visit, as is the churchyard with its ninety-nine yew trees and the most elaborate tombs I have ever seen. Some of them are table tombs, others are the cylindrical type known locally as 'tea-caddy tombs'. There's a lovely lychgate here which was built with timbers taken from the belfry roof after it had been badly damaged in 1883 when lightning struck the top of the church tower, scattering masonry around – much of it on the roof of the church. The curious 'clipping' ceremony, of pre-Christian origin, is held on the first Sunday after the 15th of September, when the local children join hands and encircle the church, singing hymns as they do so. Apparently years ago, once the singing was over the children were given 'puppy dog pie', a plum pie with small china dogs in. Was it considered lucky if you had a helping with a china dog in it, I wonder? Now the children are given buns and a coin instead.

When the wool trade was at its height, there were no less than twenty-five cloth mills in the Cranham–Painswick–Stroud area. The water in the valleys enabled the manufacturers to produce good woollen cloth, and it was here that the famous Stroud Water Scarlet and Uley Blue cloth, specially made to clothe the British Army, were woven. All but five of the woollen mills have closed, but I understand that two of them still produce the scarlet cloth for army tunics.

A mill at Minchinhampton still makes Melton (woollen) cloth which is used to cover tennis balls, while another at Strachan, which is also in the Stroud valley, manufactures the green woollen baize for billiard tables. The baize is made in the traditional way, with the nap being raised with teazles – modern techniques can't produce a better finish than the teazle.

Teazles were grown commercially in areas such as Gloucestershire and Oxfordshire for use in the wool industry. As well as being used by hand, a cylinder-like machine which revolved rapidly was used in the factories. This was called a 'raising gig'. The country name for teazles is 'barber's brush' or 'barber's bush'.

Within living memory, a man called Jack Derrick, known locally as Teazle Jack, grew about ten acres of teazles each year, as part of his living. He had a smallholding in a Cotswold village called Elmstone Hardwicke, and folks can still remember seeing great bundles of teazles hanging up in his open sheds, harvesting off before being taken to the cloth mills in the Stroud valley.

We wandered back over the golf course and Painswick Beacon. Masses of butterflies were feeding on the sweet flowers of summer, and the larks still sung overhead. We walked on down the road that took us to where the car was parked. Beryl and I felt quite excited – for today we had finished half our magical journey. And I had heard that a Mr and Mrs Evans and their son lived in the nearby village of Whiteway. All three are well-known craftworkers, so I had arranged to see them and have a chat about their work.

We drove along the quiet country roads until we reached the little village, where we met Peter Evans, his wife, Joy, and their son, Alan. We were welcomed into the comfortable living-room and straightaway were offered tea, which we readily accepted. I talked to Peter first, and asked him how and why he became a maker of traditional Cotswold furniture.

'Well, in the very early 1950s I was doing a job that I didn't particularly like, so I went to a furniture-makers in Hereford to learn the craft of making the sort of furniture that William Morris made – he was the fellow who, in 1870, revived and developed many traditional crafts, particularly furniture, in the south Cotswolds. Then later on, Ernest and Sidney Barnsley and Ernest Gimson did the same sort of work at nearby Sapperton. Most wonderful craftsmen they all were, and I would like to think that in time I will be able to turn out lovely pieces of furniture as they did. We go to several craft fairs each year, and exhibitions, where we sell our work and, of course, take orders too. Selling is mostly done by word of mouth – someone buys a good piece from you, others see it and then the orders grow from there. And, of course, Joy often incorporates her work with mine.'

I asked Joy how she came to start woodcarving.

'After Alan left school,' she told me, 'I felt that I needed to do some kind of work, but it had to be something that I could do at home. I've been woodcarving for the past twenty years. Sometimes Peter gets small pieces of wood that he can't possibly use, so I take them up, look at the grain and decide what to do with that particular piece. What I like to do is to carve the local wildlife, like this owl.'

She handed me a small plaque. Every feather was delicately carved, it was so lifelike.

'Well,' Joy went on, 'he just sits up there in that tree and unbeknowingly models for me. There are several squirrels out there in the trees, too, and woodpeckers and all sorts of birds, and even mice and voles. I'm never at a loss for ideas – they are here all around me in the

Mr and Mrs P. Evans: the half 'tester' bed was made by Peter, and the carvings were done by Joy.

Alan Evans, an artist in metal, with a piece of his work.

garden. At present Peter is making a rather wonderful chest of drawers, and I'm carving a pattern on the legs.'

Out in the garden there were several pieces of beautiful forged-iron work. This had all been done by their son, Alan, who is a very talented young man. How, I asked, did he become interested in this sort of work?

'I expect it was because both my parents were creating lovely pieces of work,' he told me. 'I did train at a teacher training college, but decided that I really didn't want to teach, I needed to do something more creative with my hands. So I went to work with an old blacksmith who had a small business near Worcester. I did some smithying and then I started to make silverware and jewellery, and found that I could sell as much as I could make. But my heart was still in heavy metalwork and ironwork, and so for the past ten years that is what I've been concentrating on. A few years ago four or five of we top metal smiths were asked to submit design drawings of our work to. I won and I was given four months to make a pair of forged-iron gates for St Paul's Treasury in London, which of course was a very great honour. A week after I'd accepted the work I was asked to complete it in three months because the wedding of Prince Charles and Lady Diana was going to take place. I had to work very hard to finish it on time, but it was worth it just to have been asked to make such an important thing. Then I went to London to see that the gates were hung properly.'

What a talented family, living and working out there in that quiet, peaceful Cotswold village, making such wonderful things.

EIGHT

Stone and Fleece: Fleece and Stone

Our next trip, although we thought it had been fairly well planned, turned out to be a bit on the long side. This was entirely my fault – I'd forgotten to pack the Ordnance Survey map, and my advice on which way to go in a certain wood proved to be wrong.

We started off quite well. After parking the car in the car park at Painswick, we set off, taking the road just opposite the lychgate there. We wandered through fields and very pleasant countryside, with huge flocks of sheep all around us. Then it was on to Washbrook Farm, where we saw a farm worker, so we asked him if we were, in fact, on the Cotswold Way as we couldn't see any white spots or a signpost to direct us.

Yes, he said, we were on the right track and that if we kept going straight on ahead and into the next field – where we would see some stone barns – and over a nearby stream, that would take us on to the small village of Edge.

In places the paths were quite worn. We saw a sign on a road which read 'Scottsquar Hill', but we were still not sure if we were on the right track. Luckily we met a girl with a scooter which she was having difficulty in starting, so Beryl crossed over the road and enquired about the Cotswold Way.

'Oh, yes,' she said, 'you're all right, just go through the avenue of trees on your left, and very soon you will see a sign to Haresfield Beacon, which is about two or three miles ahead, I should think.'

Just then she managed to get her machine working, and we pressed ahead towards Haresfield.

It was early July and the weather was perfect. Never have I seen such an abundance of wild flowers, and there were butterflies everywhere – meadow browns, small heath, tortoiseshell, and hundreds of small blue. They rose up in front of us as we walked through the grass. On each side of the pathway fields of corn were ripening, there was a slight breeze, and the fields looked like gently rolling seas. The words 'The lovely laughter of the windswept wheat' kept running through my mind. I don't know where I read or heard the phrase, but it is so true – when the wind is blowing quite gently through the corn the ears touch and make a laughing, rustling sound.

A short walk along a road, and then on through more woodland until we came to a stone seat. This is reputed to be Cromwell's 'Siege of Gloucester Stone', where the great man is supposed to have sat in 1643. Finally, we walked out on to Haresfield Beacon.

The light and the shade of the leafy valleys, coupled with the glorious views from up there on the high wolds, and the day as clear as crystal, made it a most memorable moment. We wandered over to the topograph, from where we could see Cotswold Edge, and the Severn Vale spread out before us. In the field a great herd of inquisitive cows was grazing and they followed us wherever we went. We were loath to leave this splendid spot, but thought that we should press on into Standish Wood. We had decided that we would not walk down into the valley towards Randwick, but thought that we could double back into Painswick, which would most likely be as far as we would want to walk on this very warm day.

Again we wandered through the most lovely woodland – every turn of the way was magical as the hot summer day wore on. There had been some wood-clearing done and a convenient log offered a seat, so we sat there drinking it all in – the view, the woods, the walk, everything.

A bearded, cheery-faced old fellow with a little terrier dog came wandering along.

'And what ju recken you be a-doin' in these yer woods then?' he asked.

'We could ask you the same thing,' I replied, smilingly. Then we told him of our plan to walk back to Painswick, but he didn't seem to hear.

'Are you a keeper?' I enquired. That made him laugh.

'By goy no, just the opposite. I be a poacher,' he replied with a grin. Then he sat down just in front of us on another recently felled tree.

'What do you poach?' I asked him.

'Oh, anything and everything, what's going,' he said.

'Have you ever been caught?' Beryl asked.

'No. But I've come damned near to it several times, I can tell 'e,' he chuckled.

Somehow his voice seemed familiar, or was it the laugh? Suddenly it came to me. 'Did you ever live in Oxfordshire?' I asked him.

'Oh, ah,' he replied. 'Worked on a farm at Handborough for about five years before I retired, and come here – but that's all about twenty-five years ago.'

That was it. I remembered him from my potato-picking days. 'Is your nickname Shackutts?' I asked him. He nodded. I went on: 'Do you remember the time when the women used to come from Eynsham to work on Taffy's farm at Handborough potato-picking? Well, I was their ganger, and you used to help to load up the sacks of spuds onto the trailers.'

'Well, I'll be damned,' Shackutts said. 'Fancy meeting you in this yer wood after all this time. 'Course, I remember you now, and the time when you asked the foreman for another tuppence an hour for the women. And I remember what he said about you, too.'

'Oh!' I cried.

'He just said that as you was too damned brainy to be spud picking, that's all.'

'If I remember, you did a bit of poaching in those days, and wasn't the local bobby after you at one time because he reckoned as you'd shot one of the duke's pheasants?'

'Oh, ah, he was after I all right, but he never did catch up with me.'

He chatted on, remembering that particular time I'd mentioned.

'I knawed as there was plenty of pheasants up round Burleigh, so I got up early one morning and biked off up there. Oh, they birds were the plumpest most lovely fat birds as you ever did see. So I takes a pot shot at one and he went down like a stone. Quick as a flash I picked him up and the few feathers that were littered about. Then I tied the bird's legs together with a piece of string and hung him up right in the middle of a great big holly bush. Then, just in case the old bobby come on the warpath I had to cover me tracks, so I went out into the field and scuffed me feet over the grass to make out as I'd bin up there looking for mushrooms. Then I walks down the hedge a bit and picked a few crab-apples and stuffed um in me bag, then got on me bike and turned for home. Who should I meet coming towards I on his bike, but the local bobby, pedalling like hell he was. Seeing me he stopped. "Right you are," he said, getting awf his bike. "I've got you this time, turn out that bag of yours and let's see that pheasant you shot a little while ago – and it's no good you saying that you didn't, because I heard you." I tipped out me bag on the grass, all that was there was a couple of bits of string and a pound or two of bright red crab-apples. By now the bobby was looking a bit red. "Don't you try to tell me you got up this early just to pick a few crab-apples?" "That's all I got," I told him. "I don't believe you," he said, "I'm off up the road to see if I can see anything suspicious-like," and he pedalled off. 'Course, he never found nothing, and when I knew that he'd gone off into the town to make his daily report to his Super, I went and collected my pheasant.

'Then my missus was a bit worried about the feathers. "What if that bobby catches sight of a few, 'cos he's always snooping about round here – then the cat would be out of the bag," she cried. So I ses to 'er, "Why don't you burn 'um on a bonfire out in the garden?" "But what if he smells it?" she said, "'cos them feathers do stink so on a bonfire." "Tell him you be burning an old cushion that one of the grandchildren piddled on, that'll shut him up."

'And that's what she did. We had that bird for our dinner the following Sunday. Oh, he was a beauty, plump and fat and very tasty. My missus is a good cook and 'er stuffed that bird with parsley, thyme and onion stuffing. None of that yer servin' him up, like the gentry do, with the tail feathers stuck up his arse. We had baked spuds and Brussels out of me garden. Then we finished up with a lovely apple pie – Bramleys they were – I just took a few from the vicarage garden. Well, the last time I went to church he preached about "sharing and caring", so I took his advice and "shared" a few of his apples.

'Well,' Shackutts went on, looking at his pocket watch, 'I shall have to be on me way, we got a leveret pie for dinner today – I caught him yesterday, and picked a few early mushrooms to go with it, and my missus said not to be late, so I'll bid good day me dears, and good walking,' he said cheerfully. Then he whistled up his dog and set off through the wood at a fair pace.

We, too, must get on.

We reached a place in the wood that had three distinct paths – one straight on, one to the left, one to the right, and not a white spot in sight. Beryl thought that we should take the one to the left. I thought the middle one, which we settled for. After walking a good mile or more we came to the edge of the wood which led onto a lane. We peered over a field gate.

'What's that great stretch of water over yonder?' Beryl asked – it was the River Severn. We didn't realise that we were that far down country.

'More to the point,' I said, 'what's this great big town before us?' Stroud! We had definitely taken the wrong path in the wood, and were now some miles off our track.

'Shall we go back through the wood to where we took the wrong turn?' Beryl said.

The day was hot and I for one didn't feel like walking back all that way. A few houses and bungalows lay along the lane.

'What say we knock on the first door and ask if we can use the phone to get a taxi to take us back to Painswick?' I suggested, feeling quite guilty that I had led us off the straight and narrow.

A pretty front garden with bright summer flowers led to a neat looking bungalow. We knocked. A pleasant elderly lady came to the door, we told her our troubles.

'Oh, come in,' she cried. So we propped our thumb sticks outside the door and she ushered us into a bright kitchen. Then she went off, brought back the phone book and advised us on the best taxi firm. Then she took me into the hall to the phone – how trusting, we could have been anyone, robbers or con women. We told her that she really should be more careful who she let into her home.

'I've been a schoolmistress nearly all my life,' she told us. 'And I'm a pretty good judge of character. I knew that you were genuine people.'

After great difficulty I managed to get on to a taxi firm. They said that they would pick us up at the bottom of the lane in about twenty minutes. I explained how we were dressed, to make it easy for the driver to spot us.

We expressed our grateful thanks, said hello to the man of the house who was busy gardening, and walked twenty-five yards to the bottom of the lane and waited for the taxi. For three-quarters of an hour we stuck there, but no taxi came.

So we had to turn around and walk, by road, all the way back to Painswick, and it was uphill most of the way, too! Talk about being tired and weary and very, very hot by the time we finally reached the car park. We reckoned that we had walked a good ten or twelve miles that day.

That'll teach me to pack the Ordnance Survey map next time!

Beryl lost again on the way from Edge to Standish Wood.

NINE

Nor Any Other Wold Like Cotswold

The further down country we got, the further we had to drive, so that by now it was taking us a good hour to get from my home to our starting point.

On this particular day we decided that we would park at Haresfield Beacon and walk down towards Randwick and into Ryford, and then turn around and walk straight back to the car, drive back to Ryford, park the car at Stanley Mill near King's Stanley – and start walking

So that's just what we did. The walk from Haresfield Beacon to Ryeford and back again was uneventful, except that it was very hard climbing back to where the car was – but it was quite early in the morning and we were still quite fresh.

The drive in the car gave us a little rest, after which we parked at Stanley Mill and set off again. We walked for about half a mile, passing Peckstreet Farm and farm land. Up in front of us we could see the Cotswold ridge – 'That's where we have to get to,' I told Beryl. It looked very steep and thickly wooded, and that morning the hills and woods high up on the ridge had a smudgy, hazy look about them – that was a certainty that the day would be hot and sunny.

We walked out onto a road for a few hundred yards, and then turned up by a chapel and began to climb up Pen Lane. The giant pig-weed – or hog-weed, as it is known in some counties – and cow parsley was almost as tall as we were, and we literally had to fight our way through it, steadily climbing all the while. At the end of the lane we got over a stile and then into Stanley Wood. From there paths led in several different ways. We were so busy chattering that we took the one that lay straight ahead. Up and up we climbed, through a lovely green beech-wood that at least offered us plenty of shade, for the day was very hot. As we walked through the dappled sunshine, we heard the sound of wood-sawing, and after a little while we came to a big clearing where we saw a man cutting down trees. He looked

Cotswold Magic.

very surprised when he saw us. We stopped and asked him if we were on the official Cotswold Way, and told him that we were making our way to Coaley picnic site.

'No, indeed you are not,' he said, 'but if you walk straight on up ahead you will come out onto a road, turn right and about half a mile along that road will bring you out just to the picnic site. You'll see a sign pointing to it. I rather think,' he added, 'that when you entered the wood in the first place you should have turned sharp right, instead of which you must have come up the middle path.'

I took a photo of him with his protective helmet on, waved cheerio, and we pushed on ahead. Quite soon we reached a rather busy road, turned right and started plodding along it. The hot sun bore down – I should think that the temperature was in the eighties at least. I stopped and looked in my back pack for my sun hat – no luck, but there was a big white handkerchief, so I knotted it at each corner and plonked it on my head. Then I picked a couple of coltsfoot leaves from the grass verge and tucked them partly under the handkerchief at the back, which gave me wonderful cool protection on the back of my neck. This was a trick that the old farm workers used to do, only they fixed the big green leaves under their caps when they were working out in the hot fields all day, hoeing and singling sugar beet and mangolds.

We were walking single file along the busy road, sometimes having to leap onto the grass verge out of the way of fast cars and lorries. Then Beryl, who was up in front, turned around and caught sight of me with my knotted handkerchief and the green leaves, and she nearly exploded with laughter.

'Good Lord, mother-in-law,' she cried, 'whatever are you going to do next! People will think that you're mad.'

'Let 'um think,' I said. 'If they don't like what they see they must look the other way, as long as it keeps me a bit cool I don't care.'

In fact most of the car drivers seemed highly amused at this mature woman striding along, knotted handkerchief with green leaves hanging down, walking boots, thumb stick and all, and waved good-heartedly as they passed.

All along the right-hand side of the road was a continuation of the wood that we had come through, and on the left-hand side was a gliding club with gliders continually landing. Still we plodded on, and that hot sun bore down.

'Did that man say that it was half a mile along the road?' Beryl asked.

'Yes, he did, but I reckon he meant two and a half miles,' I replied.

Then Beryl stopped and asked a man who was parked in a lay-by watching the gliders, and he said that we still had at least another mile to go, although by now we'd been walking for ages.

At last we saw the sign which read 'Coaley Peak, Picnic Site'. A few more yards and we were there.

We took a look at a colourful, glass-enclosed notice board, giving all sorts of information about the area and the flora and fauna to be found there. After we had told him of our walk along the road, a kindly Cotswold warden – the first we had seen during our travels – pointed out to us just where the path through Buckholt Wood and Stanley Wood came out. He told us that it would take us back again to the Pen Lane area and eventually to the car. He also told us about the Nympsfield long barrow, open to the heavens, that lay in the next field just past the picnic site, but we had already walked a long way – it would have to wait until another time.

He wished us luck and we set off through that wood like a couple of gazelles. It wasn't a walk, more of a run, very easy going and, of course, downhill all the way! We noticed quite a few blackberry bushes full of flowers and autumn promise of a goodly crop of fruit. We came out of Buckholt Wood into a small field. Once across this we would be into Stanley Wood. But first the field, shoulder-high in stinging nettles, had to be tackled. We must have looked like soldiers when they cross rivers holding their guns above their heads to keep them dry – only we were holding our thumb sticks up, not to keep them dry, but to stop us stinging our bare hands and arms on that sea of nettles. On reaching Pen Lane, we looked around for the white spot that should have sent us right-handed through the wood in the first place. After much searching we found it. The branches of a nearby

Some shade at last.

bush had simply grown right over the spot – no wonder we hadn't seen it. Also we really shouldn't have walked up Pen Lane, so we took a sign to our right which brought us again to the road, and over a couple of fields and out again past Peckstreet Farm, and then on a little way to the car which was parked near Stanley Mill.

Before turning for home we drove to King's Stanley church; we had heard of rather an unusual epigraph to a barmaid in the churchyard there. Mind you, we began to think that we would never find it, and were beginning to make our way towards the gate when we spotted it. It is really a family tomb and there are other family names inscribed on it in copperplate. At the bottom are these words:

> 'Twas as she tript from cask to cask
> In at a bung hole quickly fell
> Suffocation was her task
> She had not time to say farewell.

The tomb is near the path on the left-hand side as you make for the gate.

We'd had another lovely day, full of fun and laughter. We found that we had both caught the sun and our arms were quite burned – that happened when we were walking along that road!

TEN

No Fairer Country Could Be Found than Cotswold Hills Where Sheep Abound

A couple of weeks later we were off again on our magical journey.

We parked the car at Coaley Peak picnic site and then walked over the next field to look at Nympsfield *open* long barrow. It gave us an idea of what Belas Knap might look like from the inside, being of the same age, but unlike Belas Knap this barrow was opened up many years ago and the skeletons and small items removed. We asked an old fellow about this and he replied, 'Well, I really dun't knaw very much about it, although I've lived hereabouts all me life, but I do knaw that all the skellintons was took away or damaged years and years ago.'

We walked on to Frocester Hill – and what a fantastic view we had from there, for the day was fine and clear and we could see May Hill and over the Berkeley Vale and away in the distance the River Severn, getting noticeably wider and wider as we journeyed along. On the hill there is a panoramic dial giving details of viewpoints and the mileage to them as the crow flies, and we spent quite a while finding out the direction of places miles and miles away. Although the day was already very warm it was fairly breezy up there, but then we were pretty high up.

We made our way through what had been a stone quarry, long since left to the birds, butterflies and flowers – in fact it is now a nature reserve. We saw several different species of butterflies, some that I'd never seen before. Suddenly a huge orangey-yellow one flew in front of us, and we tried very hard to take a picture of it. But it must have been the original 'elusive butterfly', flitting as it did from flower to flower. Just as we were about to take a picture of it, it would take off again, only to rest tantalisingly a few inaccessible yards away.

Here the rosebay willowherb, meadowsweet and giant pig-weed were surely at their best, for they were as tall – sometimes even taller

At Coaley Peak: Beryl doing her Dolly Parton act.

– than us in places. In fact, in the whole of this area, the wild flowers were growing in abundance and there was birdsong everywhere. We came to a spot called Crawley Barns, and we knew that somewhere to our left was another long barrow called Hetty Pegler's Tump. We aimed to call there on our way home, as it lies just off the Cotswold Way, and we knew that at one of the cottages at Crawley Barns we could ask for the key to this Stone Age long barrow, and have a good look round.

On and on we walked, up hill and then down, through very lovely woodland until we came to Uleybury Iron Age hillfort. This is a huge site comprising about thirty acres. Here we met lots of people out walking. Apparently walking right around the fort is a favourite occupation hereabouts. There were folk exercising their dogs, and in some cases just themselves. We met and chatted to a man and a young lad up there, and we asked the youngster if he would take a picture of us. He did, and it turned out quite well.

After we had walked right around Uleybury hillfort, we made our way to the road and then back to where the car was parked. On our way we saw a signpost to Nympsfield Village. I was so intrigued by the name that I said to Beryl, 'One day, when we have more time, perhaps we can pop down there.' Its name was so very different to those of any other places around that I felt I must go and see it some time. After a little refreshment – we always bring coffee and some homemade cakes with us to eat when we get a bit peckish or, as my mother used to say, 'eat a little bit, just to keep the worms alive' – we drove along the B4066 to the turn to Uley village and parked the car. We didn't go down to the village – that again would have to wait until another time – but made our way in the opposite direction, back up onto the Cotswold Way. We walked through a small wood and out on to Cam Long Down. And what a walk it was, too. Very hilly, but worth it for the wonderful views over miles of rolling countryside – breathtakingly beautiful is the only way to describe them. I know that I keep writing about them, but until you have walked along the Cotswold Way, you have no idea that there are such fantastic views – you would never see such beauty from the roadway, and definitely not if you were travelling by car.

All over Cam Long Down there are lots of funny ridges and bumps. Some say that these odd bumps are called pillow mounds, built to encourage rabbits to take up residence there – I never thought rabbits needed any encouragement to set up house anywhere, but that's how the story goes! Another legend about how Cam Long Down was formed – because it is certainly very different from the other Cotswold hills around – comes from Lewis Wiltshire's book *The Vale of Berkeley*. The Devil had taken a dislike to Gloucestershire because of the numerous churches to be found there, so he decided that he would try to flood the county by damming the River Severn, and so drowning all the people living there. To carry out such a great task he needed plenty of stones, and finding a quarry above the hills at Dursley that would provide him with all the material he needed, he started filling his giant wheelbarrow with a very big and heavy stone. After journeying a little while he sat down to rest, for the day was hot and the wheelbarrow became heavier and heavier to push. While he was taking his ease, a cobbler came along from the opposite direction. Strung on his back was a string of worn-out boots and shoes which he was going to take home and repair. The cobbler stopped and chatted to the Devil, who asked him how far it was from the River Severn. The cobbler, smelling a rat, pointed to the mass of worn-out shoes on his back, and said that he had worn them all out on his journey from there. The Devil, realising what a long way it was and that he would have to make several journeys to dam the river, changed his mind about his grudge against the Gloucestershire churches and promptly tipped his huge wheelbarrow full of stones out – and that was how Cam Long Down came to be formed.

On we walked to Cam Peak. Then it was downhill travelling for a time. After a little while we reached Downhouse Farm and soon came to the lovely little town of Dursley, which is surrounded by enchanting countryside and a soft-flowing river. We must both have been losing pounds in weight for the perspiration ran off us like water off a duck's back. Nestling under Stinchcombe Hill – another steep way, which we would have to climb on our next trip – the town was once a busy centre for the wool and cloth trade, and although the majority of these businesses have long since disappeared, it can boast that it is, in fact, the home of the famous Lister engines. Well over a hundred years ago, one man and a boy started the firm of Lister in a shed: now they employ 1500 people and the engines are famous all over the world.

Dursley is dominated by the lovely market house with a beautiful hipped roof and an imposing statue of Queen Anne. We found a small café where we drank several cups of strong hot tea, which of course made us hotter than ever. We also stuffed ourselves with buttered teacakes, as if we'd had nothing to eat all day. Beryl asked the proprietor if she knew of any way that we could get a lift back to where we'd parked the car. She said that if we could hang on for a bit she might be able to fix up something with a delivery lorry driver who would be calling within the next half-hour – that is, if we could wait that long.

Neither Beryl nor I were in that much hurry, and we needed no excuse just to sit in the window seat and watch the world go by. It must have been one of the hottest days so far – nearing the eighties, I would think.

The lorry driver arrived at the café with a supply of groceries for the owner. She must have mentioned that we could do with a lift, for he turned around and grinned and said that he wouldn't be long. Such a nice fellow he was, too, helping us into the high cab and chatting away nineteen to the dozen as we sped along, until we spotted the car. 'I shall have to get my missus to go on a walking trip,' he said, grinning at us, 'you both look so fit and healthy.' We thanked him, and he sped off in the direction of Painswick. It was true, we both looked the picture of health. It was all that exercise, fresh air and sunshine, and the fact that we were enjoying every minute of our trip.

Goodness knows how many miles we walked on that day – getting on for ten, I would think. Beryl said that it felt like twenty! But we still had some exploring to do. So we drove along the road a little way and then stopped at a cottage to pick up the key to Hetty Pegler's Tump, which was situated less than a quarter of a mile away. We came to a sign which read 'Uley Tumulus – Ancient Monument' – in other words, Hetty Pegler's Tump!

The name derives from Hetty, wife of one Henry Pegler who had owned the field in the seventeenth century. The Stone Age long barrow has apparently been opened several times over the centuries and items of interest taken away to museums.

Up the side of a field we walked until we reached the entrance to the long barrow. Beryl wouldn't venture in. Mind you, there wasn't a lot to see, for it was very dark in there, and if I'd had a torch maybe I could have seen more. But I did get a rather eerie feeling in there – to think that I was in a burial chamber of folk who lived thereabouts between 4000 and 5000 years ago! From somewhere I could hear the drip, drip of water plopping onto the stone slabs. It was cold and clammy, and I was quite glad to come out into the hot sunshine – and the twentieth century!

We wandered back down the field again. In the hedgerows the early blackberries were beginning to change colour, and the corn in the

Kissing-gate at Uley Tumulus, or Hetty Pegler's Tump.

fields had started to ripen. I said I thought that the harvest would be much earlier than usual because of the very hot summer.

We returned the key to the little box outside the cottage door, and then made our way home, after another lovely day.

Later on in the year I was asked to open a Cookshop in Dursley and the road where the shop is situated actually lies along the Cotswold Way. I had a super day there and afterwards was able to see much more of the town, but not before we had had lunch at the shop-owner's in-laws' delightful house, so remote I'm sure I couldn't find it again. The view over the valley was superb. They pointed out a deserted mansion on the other side of the valley – and one day I'll try to find it.

Map 4

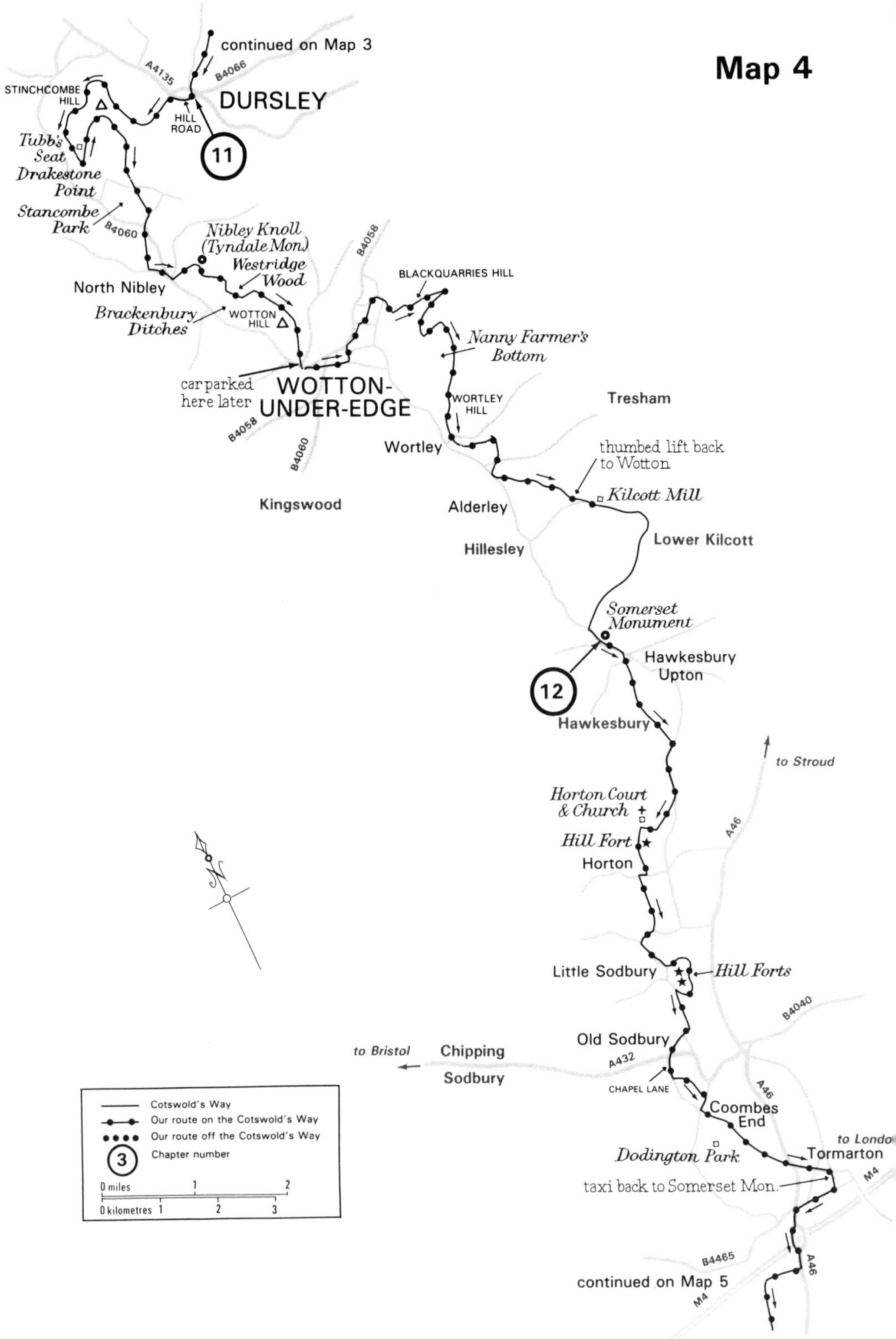
continued on Map 3
A4135
B4066
STINCHCOMBE HILL
DURSLEY
HILL ROAD
11
Tubb's Seat
Drakestone Point
Stancombe Park
B4060
Nibley Knoll (Tyndale Mon)
Westridge Wood
B4058
BLACKQUARRIES HILL
North Nibley
Brackenbury Ditches
WOTTON HILL
Nanny Farmer's Bottom
car parked here later
WOTTON-UNDER-EDGE
WORTLEY HILL
Tresham
B4058
B4060
Wortley
thumbed lift back to Wotton
Kilcott Mill
Kingswood
Alderley
Lower Kilcott
Hillesley
Somerset Monument
Hawkesbury Upton
12
Hawkesbury
to Stroud
Horton Court & Church
A46
Hill Fort
Horton
Little Sodbury
Hill Forts
B4040
Old Sodbury
to Bristol
Chipping Sodbury
A432
CHAPEL LANE
A46
Coombes End
Dodington Park
to London
Tormarton
taxi back to Somerset Mon.
M4
B4465
A46
continued on Map 5
M4
Cotswold's Way
Our route on the Cotswold's Way
Our route off the Cotswold's Way
3
Chapter number
0 miles 1 2
0 kilometres 1 2 3

ELEVEN

Earth Has Not Anything to Show More Fair

(Wordsworth)

The great poet could have easily been writing about the Cotswolds, as we set out very early on a lovely warm summer morning. All around the fields of corn were ripening fast, cattle and huge flocks of sheep were grazing contentedly up on those high wonderful wolds, and there were a few soft clouds in the otherwise blue sky. We were now entering an area of quaint old mills and ancient monuments, surrounded by ever-changing countryside.

Our starting point was Dursley, which we reached in very good time. We parked the car in the town's car park, and set off at a goodly pace up May Lane and on to Hill Road towards Stinchcombe Hill. The walk was very steep and within a few minutes we were looking back at the lovely grey town lying peacefully below. Soon we reached the peak of Stinchcombe Hill and the golf course up there, and Beryl remarked, 'It's strange that super healthy spots in the Cotswolds are always chosen for golf courses!' The Way went around it, and then on right to the edge of the hill, where there is a stone shelter. There is a memorial stone in the shelter, which reads: 'This shelter was erected by the trustees of the Stinchcombe Hill Trust with the assistance of the Rural District Council, and of the Stinchcombe Hill and Dursley Golf Clubs as a further tribute to the memory of Sir Stanley William Tubbs (Bart.), who, having provided facilities for these Clubs, gave the land on Stinchcombe Hill in trust to the public for ever. MCMLIV.'

This shelter is situated at a very high point – we were almost 700 feet up – with sweeping views in front and to either side of this curiously T-shaped hill. There again was the great, wide ribbon sweep of the River Severn, and across to our right the Forest of Dean, looking thick, black and foreboding. We could even pick out the Somerset Monument near Hawkesbury Upton, some ten miles away, and the Brecon Beacons rising up clear and appearing so close on that perfect

Memorial shelter on Stinchcombe Hill.

summer morning, for it was still only nine o'clock! Down below, the village of Stinchcombe nestled in the valley.

We walked on a bit further to Drakestone Point, which was even higher than Stinchcombe Hill, and again we were absolutely bewitched with the panoramic view. After getting our breath back, we pressed on: the walk thankfully went downhill slightly, and in a little while we passed through the edge of Stancombe Park, which was looking very lovely. The trees were heavy with summer leaf, and out in the open spaces there were plenty of wild flowers blooming – foxgloves, honeysuckle and masses of tall rosebay willowherb. The air was filled with the quiet hum of bees, and the sweet heady smell of summer was everywhere.

Soon we reached the roadway and the village of North Nibley, which lay very quiet in the morning sunshine. On we went up to Nibley Knoll and out onto another high peak to the Tyndale Monument, which was erected in 1866 as a memorial to William Tyndale, the translator of the Bible. He was born in the 1490s. We later learned that he received his MA at Oxford and in 1521 moved to Little Sodbury where he appears to have been tutor and chaplain to Sir John Walsh, who lived at the manor there. Once William Tyndale was heard to remark, 'If God shall spare my life, before long the boy that follows the plough shall know more about the Bible than the Pope.' So in 1530 he began his translation, but because of the troublesome religious period that the country was going through at that time, he was charged with heresy and his body burnt at the stake in 1536. Strangely enough, two years later King Henry VIII decreed that every child should have an English Bible.

But we didn't climb the Tyndale Monument. We had planned to do an extra few miles walking that day, so we conserved our energy for later on. There was a large party of schoolchildren frolicking about near the tall column, evidently out for a day's history lesson.

Following the path through banks of woodland, with the trees clinging on to the steep hillsides, we reached Westridge Wood. From there we walked on to Brackenberry Ditches, another ancient hillfort. The whole area was covered with trees and small bushes, and the only

The Tyndale Monument.

sound up there was the singing of blackbirds and robins, and there were butterflies everywhere.

Now the way was all downhill through a wooded glade to Wotton Hill, and soon we reached the lovely little town of Wotton-under-Edge. Wotton was once famous for its wool trade, and there were several cloth mills along the river there. A census taken early in the seventeenth century showed that at least half of the town's population were employed in the clothing trade. But, sadly, like many of the wool towns in the Cotswolds, Wotton-under-Edge had started to decline by the early nineteenth century – but, like other towns, it survived, and is now a very prosperous place.

Wotton-under-Edge has a great place in history, for Isaac Pitman, who invented the shorthand system, lived there for many years, and there is a plaque on his old house in Orchard Street to that effect. We lingered long in Wotton for there is much to see, and many fine old buildings in the town. Sixteenth-, seventeenth- and eighteenth-century cottages and houses line the streets. There is also a tolsey – where, in the old days, a toll had to be paid – and a beautiful town hall. We peeped into the cool church of St Mary the Virgin, famous for its memorial brasses to the Berkeley family, and for its lovely organ, which was once housed in St Martins-in-the-Fields in London where it was often played by Handel but it was put up for sale in 1799 because it was said to be in a poor condition. It was bought and installed in Wotton church a year later.

Out into the brilliant sunshine again. We sat for a while and rested on a seat from where we hoped to catch a bus back to Dursley. An elderly couple were already sitting there, and of course we started chatting. They, too, were waiting for the bus. It appeared that they lived in an isolated farm cottage, down a lane somewhere between Wotton-under-Edge and Dursley, and that their names were Mabel and Bert Woodman. 'We comes in once a week to do our shopping,' Mabel said, pointing to the four bulging, shiny rexine shopping bags at their feet. Then Bert started chatting away nineteen to the dozen. I suppose living up in the fields somewhere they got a bit lonely, and were glad to have a chat to anybody.

'Hark at him,' Mabel cried, 'and they ses we women can chatter.'

But that didn't stop him, he talked about their family, now all left home, and about his garden where they grow all the vegetables and fruit they need.

'And now we got the electric *and* a water lavatory,' Bert went on. ''Course we had one of them earth ones right away from the house for years.'

'Oh, did you,' I replied, laughing, 'I know all about them.'

Then the penny dropped. Mabel had heard Beryl call me Mollie.

'You ent the one as writ all about 'm are you?' she said. 'I read about a Mollie somebody as found out all about them earth ones, don't you remember, Bert, I said at the time 'er wants to come and see owern 'cos we hadn't got our water one then.'

'Yes,' I said, 'I was the very one,' and we had a good chuckle about it. Then Bert told us a very funny story. 'This only happened a few weeks ago,' he went on. 'You see, we hadn't had ower water closet long, when my old uncle who lives over in Alderley lost his missus, so we asked him if he'd like to come over and stay with us for a week or so. He'd bin over before, but not since ower new water closet was set up just outside the back door.

'When we first had it my missus asked the farmer's wife what 'er should clean it with, we not being used to havin' to do that, you see. The farmer's wife said, "Well, if you haven't got any special lavatory cleaner, just pour some paraffin oil down the pan, that'll clean it." So, with my uncle a-comin' and 'er wanting it all to look nice and clean, 'er done just that and poured a good lot of paraffin down the lavatory, just before my old Uncle Charley arrived. First thing he wanted to do was to go to the privy, and he went to go off down the garden. We stopped him and said that we had got one nearer to the house now. In he went and, as usual, lit his old pipe dropping the match in the pan – old men always smoke thur pipe in them places. Suddenly, thur was the biggest bang as you ever heard, and out comes my Uncle Charley with his trousers down round his ankles, braces dangling along the ground, and walking very funny-like. "Bugger me," ee ses, "thas the last time I etts pickled onions for breakfast."'

Just then the bus came along, and we all trooped on. It was rather crowded so that we were unable to sit near to Mabel and Bert, which was a pity, we might have heard a few more tales.

When they got off they turned and waved a cheery goodbye. I noticed a farm lying across the fields some way away, and I suppose their cottage was somewhere beyond that.

Beryl and I were still chuckling about Bert's story when we got off the bus at Dursley. Only then did we realise that we had been so taken up with his story that we had forgotten to take a photo of those two delightful country folk. And it was then that I remembered when we were young, our mother used to use paraffin oil for quite a lot of cleaning in the house, for one thing it was good for was getting rid of grease, and another, when we caught head lice our mother always washed our hair with it to get rid of them.

It was about two o'clock, so we decided that we'd pick up the car and drive back to Wotton-under-Edge and try and get a few more miles' walking in. The day was quite warm but we knew that much of the walk would be through woodland so it wouldn't be too bad – and I'd remembered to pack my sunhat.

Back at Wotton-under-Edge we parked the car and started walking up Sinwell Lane and on to Lisleway Hill, steadily climbing all the while, to Blackquarries Hill. From up there we noticed how very much the countryside was changing. Gone were the very high hills, now the hills were smaller, more rounded, and the downland country had a softer look about it. Even the woodlands seemed different, not so bold looking as they had been on our earlier walks. The views were still beautiful, just different. We even picked out the Mendip Hills from this point.

Then the way dipped down across fields and woodland until we came to an area called Nanny Farmer's Bottom. It just seemed to be a sweep of fairly coarse grassland, and I suppose once it had belonged to a lady of that name. We came out onto a green lane down Wortley Hill which eventually brought us to the village of Wortley – well, at least to some farm buildings which lay on the outskirts of the village. Coming down the lane to our left were a couple of men, one young and the other much older. Of course, we stopped and chatted to them. The young man was very quiet and left it to the older one to chat to us. I discovered that his name was Melvo – Melvo William Taylor – and that he had lived in Wortley village for the past twenty-five years.

'I was born in the nearby village of Horsley,' he told me, 'there were thirteen of us in the family, eight girls and five boys. My father was an unqualified vet, he never had any training, but he was as good as any qualified man.

'When I left school I worked for some time in a local factory, then when the war broke out I joined up and went into the army and served in Italy and Greece – I was wounded when we were fighting in Italy.'

'What did you do after you were demobbed?' I enquired.

'Oh, I did a bit of timber felling on the big estates round here, mind you I never had any training for it, but I worked with the old fellows and learned the know-how that way. It was the same with dry-stonewalling, just by watching the old 'uns I became a very good stone-waller. So then I became self-employed and took jobs as a skilled waller and a timber feller for years.

'I bought an old mill several years ago, just in the next village. It was going cheap, 'course it had been empty for years and years. Apparently the last thing it had been used for was a timber mill and there was a marvellous wood saw there – it was four feet in diameter and it was powered by a water wheel. Mind you,' he went on, 'I've been retired some years now, that's how I come to be walking out in the sunshine at eleven o'clock in the morning.

'Some time ago one of my friends said he'd got a lot of apples that wanted picking, so me and my old mate said that we'd pick 'um for him. "Pick the ones on the lowest branches first," he said.

'Well, we stood there picking away when suddenly I was hit on the backside that hard I pitched ass-over-head a couple of times before landing on the grass a few feet away from the apple tree. I was just about to ask my mate what the hell he thought he was up to when he joined me. Unbeknown to us there were two rams grazing in the orchard, and it was one of them that had attacked us. We told the owner to take the damned things out otherwise he'd have to pick his own apples.

Mr Melvo Taylor and friend talking to Beryl.

'But this is a lovely quiet little village, there's only eighteen houses here. Most of the land around used to belong to a big estate but that was split up some time ago. Mostly it's farming round here, that's where several of the men are employed, on the farms. There's quite a good bus service that goes into Dursley. I can catch one just down the bottom of this lane and go and do my bit of shopping.

'Ah,' he said, looking round at the lovely countryside, 'this 'ull do me for the rest of my life. I got my health and strength and all this,' he said, sweeping his arm round, 'what else could anybody ask for?'

There was a rather unusual stile there, leading to Alderley – our next port of call – so we all had our photos taken there before pressing on.

It was a lovely warm day, so warm that Beryl reckoned she was getting burned by the sun. Reluctantly we said goodbye to our Wortley friends, and made our way over a flat green field and over a stile until we came to a delightful stone bridge over a small stream. The stones on the bridge were almost covered with moss and lichen, and there were clumps of bushes and trees all round and the whole area was wrapped in the slumbrous heat of the afternoon sun. It was so quiet and peaceful, and we seemed to be miles from anywhere.

Up a steep lane for a little way, and we came to the village of Alderley. We walked straight through this rather enchanting little place and, keeping to the Cotswold Way, we went over more fields and down leafy lanes. Suddenly we heard a squealing and rushing of small animals up on the bank: we had disturbed a litter of about a dozen little pink piglets who had been sleeping until we came along. They tore away across the field at such a rate that there was no time to get the camera out. This lane led to Kilcott Mill which we reached after a little while. The Somerset Monument, which we had hoped to reach today, looked a long way off. We were both beginning to feel a bit weary and somehow we had to get back to Wotton, so we turned tail and walked back up the lane again. No sign of the piglets this time, so we made our way onto the road and began to wonder how in the world we were going to get back. We started walking towards Wotton. The road was fairly steep and winding and quite busy with

Another mile, another stile.

the traffic. After a little while, Beryl said, laughingly, 'What's the matter with your thumb then, out of action, is it?' So, out went the right arm and thumb, and in a moment a car pulled up in front of us. A woman got out and met us.

'I'm going into Wotton to pick up my son from school,' she said. 'Would you like a lift as far as there?'

Yes please, we cried, that was just where we wanted to get to. We went to get in the back. She stopped us, saying, 'Oh, could one of you sit in front, I've got the baby in the back' – and snuggled down, fast asleep, was her three-month-old daughter. Her mother seemed very interested in what we were doing. 'Perhaps,' she said a little wistfully, 'I'll be able to walk the Cotswold Way when the family have grown up.'

She dropped us right at the car park. She would have a surprise when she got home. I had sat in the back of the car with the baby and I was so grateful to her for stopping that unbeknown to her, I had got out one of my paperback books from my back pack, quickly scribbled my thanks in it and left it on the seat.

A few weeks later I had a letter of thanks from her. She had written to the publishers to find out my address: they were reluctant to give it to her until she told them why.

What lovely folk we had met that day, and we reckoned we had walked about twelve or fourteen miles.

Fellow travellers.

TWELVE

Sweeping Valleys and Green Woodlands

Today, as we journeyed towards our starting point, we noticed that the corn harvest was in full swing. Everywhere giant red combines were creeping over the hills and vales harvesting the precious grain. In other fields huge round straw bales waited to be carted away – and in some places where the whole harvest had been cleared, great red smoking fires raged over the countryside where farmers were stubble-burning.

Our plan had been to walk about a mile from Kilcott Mill to Lower Kilcott and then on to the Somerset Monument, or Hawkesbury Monument as it is sometimes called. But when we got near to Kilcott Mill it was impossible to do that short stretch because of a field fire. We didn't think that it was worth risking life and limb by trying to walk that piece, and we knew that we would have to park the car somewhere fairly near – and that again would be too risky.

So we drove straight on up to the Somerset Monument, parked the car there, and then I went along to the cottage nearby to collect the key so that I could walk up the 140 steps to the top! Beryl, who dislikes heights, declined to join me, and she sat in the car while I trudged to the top. And what a climb! But it was worth it for the views.

I hollered down and waved to Beryl. It is said that as many as six counties can be seen from up there. As I didn't really know what I was looking for I couldn't pick them out, but since the day was very clear I could see for miles and miles.

The Monument was erected in 1846, in memory of General Lord Robert Edward Henry Somerset, a member of the Beaufort family, who – among many other things – fought at the Battle of Waterloo. There is a huge stone plaque at the bottom of the tower which gives a much more detailed account of this distinguished soldier.

We left the car there and walked on to the village of Hawkesbury

Upton. However, immediately on entering the village, the Cotswold Way veered off sharply to the right by the village pond, so we didn't see much of Hawkesbury Upton at all. The Way meandered through several fields and over two or three stiles. Everywhere the farmers were working non-stop to gather in the harvest. Eventually we reached Horton church and Horton Court, set apart from the village. Horton Court is open to the public on Wednesdays and Saturdays in summertime and it is reputed to be one of the oldest inhabited houses in the country. But it was not open to the public on the day we visited the area. Perhaps we can come back here one day when we haven't miles to walk afterwards.

Here the Cotswold Way marking was very good, and pointed the way over a couple of fields to Horton. We walked straight through the village and on across more fields, passing another hillfort, and on to Little Sodbury. We called at a shop for ice cream, for again it had become swelteringly hot. High on to our left were the Iron Age Sodbury hillforts. Columns of black smoke were billowing down, which meant that there was more stubble-burning going on – so again we gave that short piece of walk a miss.

But we did have a quick look at the charming little church there, and learned that it is dedicated to St Adeline, the patron saint of Flemish weavers, many of whom came to the Cotswolds at the height of the wool and cloth trade. This is why there are places around there with names like Petty France and Dunkirk. We walked down the road through Old Sodbury, then across the A432 and on down Chapel Lane and Coombes End.

Here the Way wasn't very clearly marked – one white spot denoted that we should go over a field gate, but the map read straight ahead. We were leaning on the gate trying to make up our mind what to do when we noticed a small woodyard just inside the gateway. Just at that moment a rather angry-looking man with an axe in his hand appeared from one of the houses on the other side of the road. I didn't like the look of the axe so we moved off down the lane a bit quick, noting that the poor man had a wooden leg.

'Where do you think he's going?' Beryl asked, very seriously, and I

– *very* unkindly – answered, 'I reckon he's going to chop a bit off his wooden leg.'

Just at that precise moment we heard the sound of wood-chopping coming from the field, and we fell about with peals of laughter. Not at the poor man's affliction, I might add, but because the wood-chopping had started the moment that I had spoken.

Just before we reached the end of the lane we stopped and chatted to a couple of men and a dog. We took some photos of them, and told them where we were making for, and they were very helpful in directing us to Dodington Park, the next stage of our walk. But we were getting a bit weary – which was a good excuse to stay for a while and chat. One of the men said that he was a retired farmer, and told me:

'Well, I'm Stanley Sherbourne and this is my friend, Gordon, we often leans on this gate and has a chatter to whoever comes by. Quite a lot of folk walks along the Cotswold Way and, of course, if they're on the right road they have to pass here.'

Any excuse for a chat: Mollie talking to Mr Sherbourne and friend.

'Have you been farming all your life?' I asked him.

'Oh yes, you see my father came to this village from Devon in the 1920s, and bought the manor farm, just next door to where we live now. That manor house is a listed building and of course very old, as you can see.'

We looked at the mullion windows and lovely stonework.

'But of course it got far too big for just my wife and myself, so I sold it and had this here bungalow built, but I kept the farmland. Because, you see,' he went on, 'I have never really retired. At the moment I've got about thirty head of beef cattle that I'm fattening up.'

I noticed that he had his big barn full up with hay and straw.

'Oh, yes, it's been a super year for all the harvesting, no trouble at all, just day after day of lovely sunshine. 'Course, you know, we farmers have always got something to moan about. With the weather being so hot and no rain, as you might say, the grass don't grow very well, so we shall have to start using the hay for feeding much earlier than usual. Then come winter, we might get a bit short of fodder.

'Still,' he went on, 'we can't have everything we wants, can we?'

His friend Gordon hadn't much to say, but we did enjoy chatting to them, and we were grateful for the rest, too.

But we said that we would have to press on.

'Would you like to come and have a cup of coffee?' Farmer Sherbourne asked.

We thanked him kindly, but said no – it would probably make us hotter than we already were.

'You just cross over the road up there,' Gordon said. 'You'll see the footpath sign by a gate, straight ahead, and you will soon be right in Dodington Park.'

We left them leaning on the gate in the sunshine.

The next part of our walk was delightful, not for the views because in this area the countryside is rather flat, but with cool grass to walk on and plenty of nice shady trees to wander under, it was really quite enjoyable.

Across the fields and through the stiles: in Dodington Park.

Harvest time in Dodington Park.

The Fountain of Life at Tormarton.

We couldn't see Dodington Park as the Way skirted around it. After walking for almost an hour and crossing over two or three stiles, we came on to the busy A46, crossed over, and after walking over another field reached the lovely Cotswold village of Tormarton. In the centre of a cluster of cottages was what had been the village water supply – a big stone fountain with the following inscription carved out on the stone: 'For the benefit of the inhabitants of Tormarton. This fountain was erected and the water supply brought from Bidwell Spring by Barbara Charlotte wife of the Rev S. M. Anderson, Rector of Tormarton. MDCCCLV.'

What a wonderful thing it must have been for these villagers to have a central place to fetch their water from. I imagine there must have been lots of chatter there, especially on a Monday morning with the housewives pumping up bucket after bucket of water to do the weekly wash.

We stopped and asked a lady who was out walking with her dog, if there was anyone in the village who did taxi work. We knew that we had walked so far across country that we would never be able to hitch a ride directly back to the Somerset Monument.

She told us of a man recently retired who did a bit of private taxi work, so we called on him and he was only too willing to take us back to our starting point. He was a quiet man who hardly spoke at all. But it was nice to sit and have a comfortable ride back, for we must have covered at least six or seven miles in the sweltering heat.

Because of holidays ahead, we thought that we must get as much walking in as possible, and so we decided to continue our walk along the Cotswold Way the next day.

We were now only about twenty-two walking miles from Bath, so our journey by car was getting longer and longer.

We parked in a lay-by along the A46 and made our way across the fields to Dyrham Park. All around us the harvest was going on, for now we were into early August. But there was still much corn to be cut, and the golden fields shimmered like sands in the bright summer sunshine. The early autumn flowers were blooming, too, and we saw

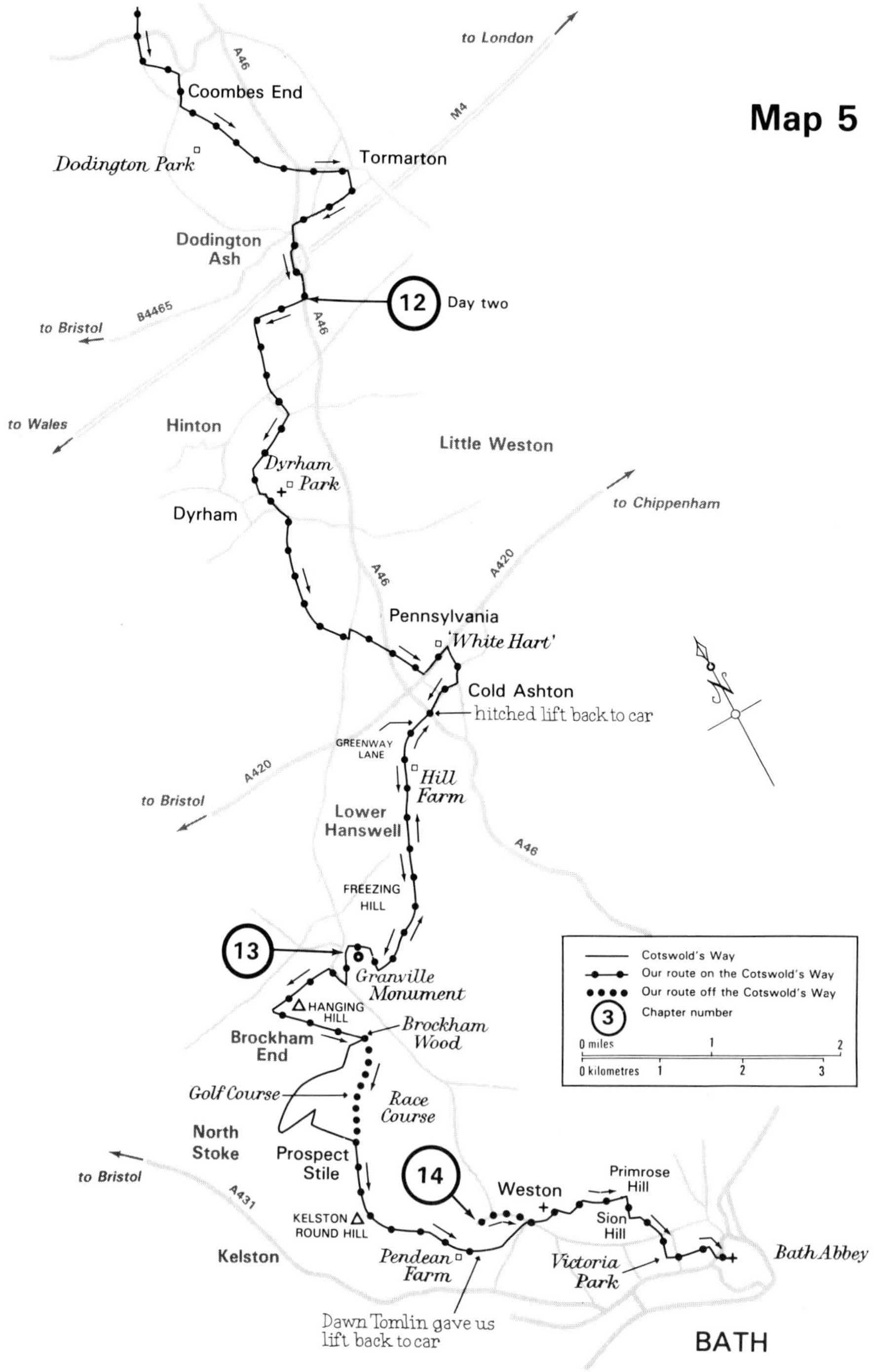
Map 5
to London
A46
M4
Coombes End
Dodington Park
Tormarton
Dodington Ash
12
Day two
B4465
to Bristol
A46
to Wales
Hinton
Little Weston
Dyrham Park
Dyrham
to Chippenham
A420
A46
Pennsylvania
'White Hart'
Cold Ashton
hitched lift back to car
GREENWAY LANE
Hill Farm
A420
to Bristol
Lower Hanswell
A46
FREEZING HILL
13
Granville Monument
HANGING HILL
Brockham End
Brockham Wood
Golf Course
Race Course
North Stoke
Prospect Stile
to Bristol
A431
14
Weston
Primrose Hill
Sion Hill
KELSTON ROUND HILL
Kelston
Pendean Farm
Victoria Park
Bath Abbey
Dawn Tomlin gave us lift back to car
BATH
Cotswold's Way
Our route on the Cotswold's Way
Our route off the Cotswold's Way
3
Chapter number
0 miles
1
2
0 kilometres
1
2
3

many blue-grey scabious, bright purple knapweed and glorious yellow toadflax on the grass verges. But there was not much birdsong, only the monotonous call of the wood pigeons, which I have always thought sounds as if they are saying 'my toe bleeds, Betty, my toe bleeds, Betty'. Listen carefully, and you might imagine that's what they are calling with their 'whoo, whoo, whoo, whowho'.

We didn't go to Dyrham House, but we did linger in the village and the church a little while. Then, keeping strictly to the Cotswold Way, we skirted the park, over hunting gates, and stiles, until we reached Pennsylvania, and finally out onto the A46 again. Here we had to do another bit of road walking, along to the White Hart Inn, and then to the village of Cold Ashton. We walked around the village and passed the beautiful manor house there, and for once saw no one to chat to. The walk that day seemed to be just straight walking, and although it was once again remarkably warm we got on very well.

Beryl always has the Ordnance Survey map in her hand and directs us along the right pathways and byways. We had certainly learned our lessons in those early days of our journey when we got lost and took wrong turnings. Now we had become quite experienced walkers.

Once again we had to cross the busy A46 and get on to Greenway Lane. Here we were quite high up, but still on a small roadway. We passed the picnic site and pressed on to Hill Farm, where we found that we were 500 feet up. There were several more fields and stiles and gates to negotiate, and we started to drop down into a green valley quite quickly. We walked through a small, cool beech wood. Its green shade was very welcome, but all too soon we came out into the brilliant sunshine. In the distance we could see more billowing smoke from stubble-burning, but thankfully it was some miles away.

We crossed yet more fields, keeping our weather eye on some distant barns that we had to make for. It was sweltering hot again, and I now carried a fan with me, which I often used. All the same, the perspiration simply dripped off us as the long hot summer day went on. Yet that very day we had passed a spot called Freezing Hill!

The Way dipped down sharply again, only to rise after a mile or so – these, of course, are the beginning of the soft, undulating hills of

Somerset. Then, suddenly, in front of us was our goal for the day.

The Granville Monument was erected in memory of Sir Bevil Granville, who fought the bloody battle of Landsdown there in 1642 in the war between the Parliamentarians and the Royalists. Granville was badly wounded, and died later at Cold Ashton. His cousin had the Monument erected in his honour.

After we'd had something to eat, we decided to make our way back. We had walked far enough that day, and we still had to get back onto the main road and try for a lift.

So we retraced our steps back over the fields to Greenway Lane, and soon we were out on the A46 once more. We felt quite safe hitch-hiking – there were two of us, and we had our thumb sticks which we could whack anyone on the head with if they got a bit fresh.

It was no trouble to get a lift. We had not been walking two minutes – mind you, I did have my thumb stuck out – when a large black limousine pulled up. 'Hop in the back, girls,' a very cultured voice called out, and the driver leaned over the driver's seat and opened the back door for us.

'Where do you wish to go?' he asked. We told him.

'No trouble at all, it's on my way home.'

We explained what we were doing, and the difficulty in getting back to the car each time.

'Jolly good way to see the countryside,' he went on, 'I must say you both look the picture of health, it must be doing you the world of good.'

The car was huge, and the back seat where we were sitting was very wide, and the last thing in comfort. We could stretch our weary legs right out. The engine purred along very smoothly and we soon reached the lay-by just off the main road. Our driver insisted on taking us right up to the door of the Metro. We thanked him kindly. He drove off, head slightly tilted, and gave us an almost royal wave – which set us wondering who in the world we had hitched a lift with.

THIRTEEN

The Broad-backed Hills of Somerset

It was hard to believe that we were getting so near to Bath. Just think – we had walked all that way through one of the hottest summers for many years. Today's trip was no exception – it promised to be another swelterer. We were still in the Cotswolds, but not for much longer: in front of us we could see the broad-backed hills of Somerset.

We parked the car near to the Granville Monument, and walked down the road a little way to an area which looked as if it had been occupied by the army. We cut off through a beech wood which eventually brought us out onto Hanging Hill, or Hangstone Hill as it is sometimes called, where there was an Ordnance Survey column. We leaned on this for a few minutes, and then made our way around yet another big golf course. On the hedgerows the blackberries were ripe and lush and we stopped to pick handfuls, greedily eating them – we discovered what a wonderful thirst-quencher they are. Elderberries, too, were ripening – a bit early, we thought, but that perhaps had something to do with the very hot weather we'd had. And such a crop too! Hanging like miniature grapes they were, reminding me to gather some soon to make home-made wine, which is like port if left for a year or more.

Already the blue-black sloes (fruit of the blackthorn), or 'slans' as they are called in some areas, showed great promise of a super crop – which means more wine and sloe gin to make during the coming weeks.

On we wandered – and it really was a wander, as we were not walking far that day. Had we wanted to hurry, we could have made it right into Bath but we decided to walk as far as Pendean Lane, and leave the last few miles for another day. We wanted to savour them, knowing that soon our wonderful voyage of discovery would be over.

We reached Brockham Wood. Here the Way markings were not

Yet another lovely stile, near Weston.

too good, and since we had literally 'walked out' of our Ordnance Survey map a while back, and thought it hardly worth getting another just for a few miles, we were glad that we had brought the little green book with us.

Even so, Beryl had to stop and ask a golfer if we were on the Cotswold Way, but he was not a lot wiser than us, for he sent us up the wrong hedge – apparently we should have gone towards Bath race course and starting-gate at that point. Anyhow, after a lot of side-tracking we eventually made it back onto the straight and narrow, first to the race course which brought us out at Prospect Stile. Again it was hilly and we could see part of the city of Bath in front of us.

Most of the harvest in this area had been gathered in, and brightly coloured pheasants were strutting about in the stubble – no doubt finding plenty to eat where the grain had fallen. Here and there some ploughing had been done, leaving expanses of newly turned soil looking reddish in the sunshine. After walking through more fields

Kelston Round Hill in the distance.

and hunting gates, Kelston Round Hill loomed in front of us: we found that the Cotswold Way does not go up and over it, but simply skirts around it. From then on it was downhill most of the way, with the whole of the city of Bath spread out before us.

We walked out on to the edge of a farm which was in a wonderful position perched on a hill overlooking the city. It was called Pendean Farm. We stopped and chatted to a man working there and found out that he owned it. I explained what we had been doing all through the summer, and asked him if we could park the car up there when we came to do our final stretch of the Cotswold Way, walking triumphantly into the city.

We could park the car there if we wished, with the greatest of pleasure, he assured us, and asked if we would like to come into the house and meet Dawn, his sister.

What charming people they were, too: over coffee and cakes the farmer, Des Tomlins, told me a bit about himself.

'Well, firstly, I'm not really what you would call a farmer, not yet anyhow. You see, my Auntie Mary died about a couple of years ago and left the farm and this lovely farmhouse to my sister, Dawn, and myself. Mind you, I used to work here many moons ago, but since then I've had all sorts of jobs: I was in the army, and I served in the police force. At the time that my aunt died, I was working in Bath, driving a lorry for a motor firm, delivering spare parts and that.'

'You say that you are not a farmer?' I said to him. 'But I noticed some young cattle out in the field when I came by.'

'Ah,' he went on, 'they are Dawn's. She will most likely make a better farmer than I will. She's got another six or seven in another field up on the hills that she's probably going to breed from. But I help with the feeding and cleaning out. As soon as it begins to get really cold we shall bring them down into a covered yard for the winter months. Oh, she's got laying hens, too. Mind you, my uncle and I built the big run for them – we blokes come in handy for that sort of thing! We've just had central heating put in, that was a bit parky up here last wintertime.'

'Do you get snowed in up here?' Beryl asked.

'Oh, yes. You see the lane, which is about a quarter of a mile long, is so narrow it soon gets blocked with snow. I think that it was about four days last winter before we could get out and down on to the main road. Still, when you live in a place like this you get prepared for that sort of thing – you know, plenty of food in the larder and stacks of wood at the ready, to keep a good fire going. As long as we can get out to feed the stock, we don't worry too much.

''Course,' he went on, 'the man that you should talk to lives just down below here at Landsdown Grange Farm. He's my neighbour – John Osborne, poet and farmer.'

Well, by the time we had chatted and admired the wonderful view from the farmhouse, and the farmer had taken us through the next field to show us the way that we would have to take through Weston and on to Bath, and had also stopped to show us a small permanent notice fixed on to a stile – evidently put there by lovers of the Cotswold Way – it was time for us to start making tracks for the car.

Mollie with Des Tomlins: 'My boots have taken a bashing!'

The notice on the stile simply said:

Cotswold Way
1982

M Bashford
B Reardon
M Fenton
D Fenton

Beautiful!

I agree, that one word says it all.

We took some photographs to remind us of Dawn and Des Tomlins, and the delightful Pendean Farm. Before leaving I said that I would like his neighbour's phone number to see if he would talk to me about his life of farming and poetry writing.

Dawn offered to take us right back to the Granville Monument in her car – what generosity! This is what struck us so vividly on the trip – the kindness and generosity of Cotswold people to two complete strangers.

We reached the monument, thanked Dawn very much, and set off for home.

FOURTEEN

The Last Lap – Bath Here We Come!

After all the happenings and the miles of walking, the wonderful views and meeting and chattering to all sorts of people, quite suddenly it seemed that our journey was coming to a close. So, needless to say, Beryl and I were both sad and excited as we set out for the very last lap of our walk.

We parked the car just below Des Tomlins' farm in Pendean Lane. Just as his farm lay about a quarter of a mile up a narrow lane, John Osborne's was also up another narrow lane, almost parallel with Farmer Tomlins'.

So, as previously arranged, we called on John Osborne, and what a wonderful character he turned out to be. Here was a hard-working farmer who also found time to write splendid poetry *and* give much of his spare time to singing and entertaining Women's Institute groups, older folks' clubs and the like, *and* selling his poetry books for two of his favourite charities. But first I asked him how long he had been at Landsdown Grange Farm.

'My father bought the farm in 1928 and I was born here, so it's always been my home, and I love every stick and stone and blade of grass that makes up the farm. What else could anyone wish for? Here we are quite high up on the hills, all God's lovely fresh air and sunshine around us. Splendid views, a good wife and family, and best of all, good health. And I hope I can stay here for the rest of my life.'

I let him go on.

'You see, this is a working farm. My youngest son works with me: today he's attending college, he goes one day each week, to learn about the financial side of farming. My wife, Rosemary, helps out too. Among other things she always assists with the Sunday morning milking so that our son, Michael, can have a lie-in.'

'What stock have you got?' I asked him.

'We've got fifty dairy cows as well as a hundred stock of beef cattle

John Osborne with his fiddle scarifier.

and dairy followers. And about 125 acres of grassland. Of course it's much too hilly to try and grow corn. You can get tractors on it – we have to, to get the hay in – but no way could you drive great combine harvesters over these hills, they'd topple over. Today I've been sowing some grass seed, right up on the top ridge which is adjacent to the Cotswold Way; on land as hilly as that I have to use my old "fiddle planter".'

'Do you mean a fiddle drill?' I asked him.

'No,' he replied, 'a drill is something which goes into the ground and drops the seed in. This is just like a fiddle, and to plant the seed you literally play it with a bow as you would if you were playing a tune, and that action scatters the seed. And I suppose you'd call it just that, a fiddle drill-cum-scarifier,' he added.

'Is it an old-fashioned thing, the fiddle?' I enquired.

'Well, yes, suppose it is. I bought it second-hand twenty years ago. Some of my farming friends borrow it from time to time – the ones that farm on hilly land like myself.'

'And the poetry, where does that come in?'

'There's so much beauty around here, how could anybody not feel poetical? Sometimes when I'm up on those hills, words just come to me. Another most unlikely place where I get inspiration, is when I'm waiting in the queue at Chippenham Market. You see, we go there most weeks to sell cattle and there's always a long wait before you can get into the market to unload the animals. That gives me time to think. I make a few notes, and hey presto! another poem emerges.'

'And the entertaining, what about that?'

'Well,' John went on, 'I've been a chorister in my local church in Weston for the past forty years, and I love singing. So a friend and I got together and we go all over the place entertaining. That's when I sell most of my poetry books.'

John Osborne is, indeed, a happy contented man, and I thought it quite fitting to end the interview with one of his poems – and certainly one of my own favourites – called simply 'Vriends on the Cotswold Way'.

I do spend countless hours
Workin' on them 'ills,
An' 'tis wondervul tha peace a mind
Thic atmosphere instils.

Me life be var tha richer
Vur tha time I spends up there,
Vur I 'as time ta think a bit
An' I of'en zes a prayer.

I maybe veedin' cattle
Or I maybe makin' 'ay
But I da meet zum zuper volk
As they walks thic Cotswold Way.

Vur it da hrun across them 'ills
Wi' views beyond compare,
Views what I da love, an' likes
Other volk ta share.

I've met volk up vrom Cornwall
An' down vrom London too,
Vrom Gloucestershire and Derbyshire
Vrom most tha country drew.

Vur 'undreds in the zummer time
Da zeem ta walk thic way
An' most everyone da raise thur 'and
An' pass tha time a day.

I da mind 'ow vather zed
Ta alwes vind tha time
Ta 'ave a word wi' passers by
'Cause 'tou'd 'elp tha zun ta zhine.

An' 'e were right I blumin' sure
'Cause just drew a little talk,
Many vriendships I've a made
Wi' volks on thic Cotswold walk.

We said cheerio to John and his wife, but said that we would call and see them on our way back.

The Cotswold Way took us straight over a recreation ground, and then on to a busy road which we had to cross. This was Weston, just two miles from the centre of Bath. At one time it was a separate village, but not any more. As the farmer had told us, 'These days you can't tell where Weston ends and Bath begins.'

From the High Street we walked past the church of All Saints and then on and on until we came to Primrose Hill. We crossed a road, went up some very steep steps which eventually brought us out onto Sion Hill, and skirted yet another golf course. We thought that this last bit of the Way would be easy, but it certainly wasn't. Of course much of it was road walking, and that always goes hard after the softness of the bridle-paths and fields, and the way into the city was quite hilly.

At last we reached the Victoria Park. Already some of the trees were losing their leaves and we scuffed our feet through carpets of red and gold and the unmistakable smell of early autumn was all around.

And now we began to descend and the walking was easy.

Over to our left was the beautiful sweep of the Royal Crescent, and in front of us the tall Victoria Monument. The architecture in Bath is fantastic. Georgian and Regency vying with each other, the stone buildings looking warm and glorious in the autumn sunshine.

Bath, of course, has a long, interesting and important history, but I am not going to dwell on much of that as it can be found in most history and guide books. But I was fascinated to find out about Beau Nash, a gentleman who lived there in Georgian times and who, because of his importance, was called 'The Uncrowned King of Bath'.

Apparently in his heyday he used to drive around the city in a gilded coach, pulled by six black horses, with an escort of out-riders blowing French horns. It was he who had the Assembly Rooms and the Gaming Rooms built. Bath in Beau Nash's time was the social centre of England, where royalty and the landed gentry met and gambled.

It was inevitable that the Romans, centuries before, with their love of hot baths and central heating, should find the hot springs there, and today those same springs are still gushing forth hot water.

Well, at last we reached the centre of busy, bustling Bath. There were crowds of visitors in the city, many of them in the main square, and for a few moments we stood and gazed at the magnificent Abbey and looked across the road to the Roman baths.

Talk about an anticlimax!

There were no bands, no one to welcome us or to say well done, or anything, after all those miles. I suppose really I should have carried a bottle of champagne in my back pack, then we could have swigged it there and then or squirted it over each other in our excitement.

Sensing the rather dull feeling, I said to Beryl, 'Shall we go over to that café and have a cup of coffee?'

'No,' she replied. 'We'll go straight back.'

And that's what we did.

By the time we reached the Osbornes' farm we were both feeling a bit more cheerful.

After downing several cups of tea, we took some photographs of John Osborne, one of him showing us how his fiddle drill-cum-scarifier worked. Then, very reluctantly, we said goodbye to our hosts, promising to call and see them again some time.

We drove back home still feeling a bit sad that our wonderful magical journey was over. I turned to Beryl and said, 'I shouldn't mind walking it the other way – from Bath to Chipping Campden, some time.'

'Well, you do it on your own then,' she retorted, 'I shan't attend.'

But I knew that she didn't mean it, for it had been a most wondrous time for both of us – a never-to-be-forgotten period of our lives, that

Journey's End: Beryl and Mollie at Bath Abbey.

neither of us will probably ever repeat again – and, even if we did, it would never be as exciting and magical as this had been.

Since the walk ended on that September afternoon, Beryl and I have done nothing but talk in glowing terms about the fantastic time we had – the laughs and getting lost and finding our way again.

And when the days are bright and beautiful, and the soft south winds blow butterflies into my garden, Beryl has often said – a little wistfully – to me, 'Wouldn't it be heavenly up on the Cotswold Way today?'

CONCLUSION

A Village Called Nympsfield

When we were walking along the Cotswold Way, I did so want to go down to the village of Nympsfield, which lay a little way off our route. It was the name that intrigued me more than anything, I think. Although on our walk we often strayed off the straight and narrow, we just didn't have time when we were in the Nympsfield area.

But the opportunity to go there came very unexpectedly. Just a year later, Nympsfield was celebrating the eight hundredth anniversary of the appointment of the first vicar to that parish. It was to be a gala weekend to raise money for the restoration of the church, and the whole village was turned into 'Ambridge' – the famous 'village' of the BBC's serial *The Archers*.

The three-hundred-year-old village pub, The Rose and Crown, had its old sign removed and a new one put up: 'The Bull'. The Nympsfield Village Stores and Post Office became the Ambridge Stores and Post Office, and the local convent became Jack Woolley's 'Grey Gables'. Court Farm, which belonged to Mr and Mrs Wooldridge, was renamed 'Brookfield', and many of the cottages and houses in Nympsfield were renamed after dwellings in Ambridge. Even the signposts leading to the village were altered. To complete the Ambridge theme the organisers asked for some members of the cast of *The Archers* to go along to meet the visitors and villagers, and I was one of those asked to go. The others were Bob Arnold, who plays Tom Forrest, Arnold Peters, who plays Jack Woolley and Richard Carrington, who plays the part of the vicar, Richard Adamson, and rode around in a battery car. And what a super time we all had, too.

We Archers entered the village on a horse-drawn brewery dray. We sat on bales of straw and waved to the crowd as if we were royalty, and all the while a young man was playing *The Archers*' signature tune, 'Barwick Green', on an accordion. There were all sorts of marvellous things going on – an exhibition of rare breeds of animals,

The day they changed Nympsfield into Ambridge.
Archers All: *left to right* Arnold Peters (Jack Woolley), Mollie Harris (Martha Woodford), Richard Carrington (Richard Adamson, the Vicar of Ambridge), Bob Arnold (Tom Forrest). (*Photograph by Bailey Newspaper Group Ltd, Dursley.*)

Nympsfield: the start of the race (*photograph by Bailey Newspaper Group Ltd, Dursley*).

old farm equipment, archery, and many others. Both the churches were beautifully decorated. The villagers wrote and produced a lovely little cookbook of traditional dishes, and they asked me to write the Foreword.

Because I am interested in such things, one of the highlights of those two days for me was the discovery of a smashing two-holer privy out in the garden of Court Farm, and the television cameras took shots of me sitting on it! It was a beautiful privy, and in very good condition.

I was able to have a good look around that lovely, and usually quiet, Cotswold village, where Stone Age folk had also made their homes five thousand years ago. There is a burial ground near there called Nympsfield long barrow, or Tump, where Stone Age men buried their dead. Unfortunately it was opened many years ago and the contents removed – skeletons and all. Now the long barrow is open to the heavens, but at least it gives an idea as to how these huge burial grounds were built.

Nympsfield: signing cookery books (*photograph by Bailey Newspaper Group Ltd, Dursley*).

There is a delightful little rhyme about Nympsfield, and of the folk of bygone days who lived there:

> Nympsfield is a pretty place
> Set apon a tump
> And all the folk do live apon
> Is ag pag dump.

'Ag pag', they told me, were sloes, or 'slans', as they are often called in my neck of the woods. But no one seemed to remember why they were used in suet puddings – the 'dump' in the rhyme meaning dumpling.

I reckon that 'ag pag dump' was what we know today as a 'spotted dick' – a boiled suet pudding with currants in – or a suet dumpling cooked in a cloth. And maybe the 'ag pags' were used instead of currants. Perhaps five thousand years ago there were no such things as currants to be had in Nympsfield. But whatever the reason, these days we use 'ag pags' to make sloe jelly, sloe wine or a delicious sloe gin – maybe an improvement on 'ag pag dump'!

The Most Famous Voice in the Cotswolds

I couldn't complete a book about the Cotswolds and some of its characters without writing a little bit about the man with 'the most famous voice in the Cotswolds' – Bob Arnold, known to millions as Tom Forrest of *The Archers*. He has played the part of Ambridge's gamekeeper for the past thirty-five years. Bob told me:

'When I first left school I worked for a local butcher delivering meat on a tradesman's bicycle. My parents kept the village pub and as a youngster I used to lie a-bed and listen to the old fellows singing below. In those days people had to make their own amusement, and after they'd had a pint or two, the old men would begin to sing all the old songs, and that was how I learned both words and tunes.

'Later on I became a folk singer and formed my own concert party. 'Course this was before the war, and I played in several radio plays, too.

'I served in the 1939–45 war, and then in 1951 I joined *The Archers* and have been in it ever since.

'In 1975 I made a record of several of the folk songs that I learned all those years ago, some of them quite rare, and almost forgotten until I recorded them. Needless to say, that record sold out very quickly. But, of course, that record was only the tip of the iceberg, and I've got lots and lots more old songs that haven't seen the light of day for ages.

'In 1960 I moved to Burford with my dear wife, Dorothy. Burford is only two miles away from my birthplace, Asthall. My life's hobby has been collecting Roman coins; as a lad I used simply to walk over the ploughed fields at Asthall and pick them up, and in one afternoon I found fifteen, for the valley where I lived was inhabited by the Romans, and Akeman Street runs right along the Windrush valley. And once I found a very special coin, not Roman but one that had belonged to Bodvoc of the Dobunni tribe, from about AD 40, and a very rare coin, which is now safely housed in the Ashmolean Museum in Oxford. Unfortunately neither my daughter, nor her husband, nor the grandchildren are interested in Roman coins, so a few years ago I sold them all, and they were listed as "one of the finest collections of Roman coins in the country".'

Uley Brewery Reborn

Uley village, which is about a mile from Nympsfield, was another place that lay a little off the Cotswold Way, and one that we didn't visit when we were doing our marathon walk. But when I was at Nympsfield for their eight-hundredth anniversary celebrations, I met two enterprising young men, Bill Doggett and Charles Wright, who have restarted an old brewery in Uley – actually in the same Cotswold stone building that first housed a brewery 150 years ago. Then, almost a century ago, the owner, a Mr Samuel Price, closed it down, and the building has been more or less empty ever since – save for the time when the local fox hounds were housed there!

Uley (pronounced Yuley) is a lovely Cotswold village situated in the Stroud valley, and it was here many moons ago that the famous 'Uley Blue' cloth was made. But the cloth mills, like many along that valley, closed down years ago.

It was a beautiful morning when I made my way to Uley, the woods and hills above the village looked bluey-grey, denoting that the day ahead would be warm and sunny. A wonderful smell wafted over the light summer air, tickling my nostrils – today I reckon was brewing day! I followed my nose, and there in front of me was a lovingly restored Cotswold stone building. I walked up the yard and met these two young men who had left their secure jobs to start up on their own.

'Is it brewing day today?' I asked.

'It certainly is,' Bill Doggett replied, 'come along in and see how it is done.'

Inside the brewing equipment was all very modern and up-to-date, shiny steel mash tubs, brewing vats and boilers, and everything else needed to produce this Uley bitter.

I asked Charles Wright when they started this venture of theirs.

'Well, I suppose it all began early last year. I used to drive through this village to work every day, and I knew that there had been a brewery here. One day I noticed that there was some repair work going on, so I called and had a chat with the owner, Richard Fayle, who planned to do the building up and let it off to craftworkers. So I had a word with my pal, Bill, and we decided that we would set up on our own, and that we would use the end part of the building as a small brewery. We had both worked in breweries so we knew a bit about what we were doing.'

'Of course,' Bill said, 'there was an awful lot of structural work to be done, besides setting up all the equipment for the brewing, but eventually, in September 1984, we took over, although we didn't produce our first brew until March 1985. At present we brew one day a week, and produce ten barrels of beer: that's 360 gallons. The rest of the time is spent in getting orders and delivering them.

'People seem to like our brew and we are doing very well – it certainly has a special flavour about it.'

'How do you account for that?' I enquired.

'Well,' Bill said, 'we think it's the fact that we use pure Cotswold spring water which comes from a spring in the hill up there – the same spring Samuel Price used all those years ago. Mind you, we had to have it tested and analysed to see if it was still pure. We use hops from Hereford and the malt comes from the next county. We are very fortunate in having the self-same storage cellar, in perfect condition, that Sam Price used. It has a sort of hooped roof and the temperature stays exactly the same, winter and summer; the old fellows who built it certainly knew what they were doing.'

At that moment the brewers' dray pulled by Rosie, the horse, came down the yard. They were off to make some local deliveries.

Opposite the brewery is the original blacksmith's shop where all the brewery horses were shod years ago. When Rosie needs a new shoe, Tom Nicholls the village blacksmith, who now occupies the shop, makes and fits it.

Charles Wright, the Uley brewer.

Just then a rather striking-looking man came walking up the yard.

'This,' Charles said, 'is our chief taster, Jasper Ely.'

Jasper, I discovered, keeps rare animals on his farm at Framilode, a village a few miles away. He has Cotswold sheep, Gloucester old spot pigs, and several different sorts of cattle. And as well as being chief taster to the brewery, he also takes all their waste malt which goes to help feed his animals.

On the day I called, Charles and Bill were brewing a special beer to be called 'Old Spot', which they hope will take on during the coming winter.

The brewers' dray which Rosie pulls has been beautifully restored by a carpenter and coach-builder, Andy Wright, who also has his workshop in part of the old brewery building. It was that same dray pulled by Rosie which we Archers had ridden around on at Nympsfield celebrations the year before, and the man who had played *The Archers*' theme music on his accordion was none other than brewer *extraordinaire* Charles Wright.

So the building that was empty for so long is alive again, with the sound of the blacksmith's anvil and the marvellous smell of brewing. Indeed, while I was there several of the locals came in to test the brew. They all had nothing but praise for the special 'Old Spot' Uley bitter, and I thought that it was pretty good, too. Old Sam Price who closed the brewery nearly a hundred years ago would be very proud, I'm sure.

Later I learned that the Uley brewers walked off with first prize with their 'Old Spot' beer at the Great Western Beer Festival held at Bristol in November where all the main brewers in the country enter their beers in competition – and that they took along one of Jasper Ely's Gloucester old spot sows as a mascot.

Broadcasting Walks and Talks

Occasionally Caroline Elliott, the producer of that delightful programme 'The Countryside in the Seasons' on Radio 4, joined us as we walked the Cotswold Way. We did broadcasts on the areas we were walking through, and spoke of some of the ups and downs we encountered through the seasons.

First of all, we did a winter broadcast, which was the Chipping Campden to Broadway walk. In springtime it was Hailes to Winchcombe, including Belas Knap. Summer found us at Painswick and the surrounding area, and, lastly, the autumn one was our triumphant entry into Bath.

In all the programmes I also interviewed people from these areas, but did *fresh* interviews of some of those people for this book.

Dialect words and Cotswold expressions

Kekky-handed	left-handed
Dudman	scarecrow
Dummal	stupid or slow
To quilt	to swallow
Every otherun day	every other day
Shackles	soup made from bones
Nettle tongue	a grumbling housewife
Chiddly pink or *chawdy*	chaffinch
Eckle	green woodpecker
Starbug	starling
All togged-up	dressed in Sunday best
Meljew	mildew
Baff-um-Jack	to fling the hands and arms across the chest to warm them
Belly callin' cupboard	hungry
Got to run round the house and call the cat a fool	got to hurry up and clean the house
The snow's just fithering down	when the snow is floating down gently
Just goin' round the knap	shepherd going for a stroll anywhere up slightly rising ground

Beliefs

Blue and green should never be seen
Unless there's another colour inbetween.

When we walked along the Cotswold Way we always seemed to see lots and lots of magpies. And me being a bit superstitious, I would nod my head and say 'good morning, sir' (bad luck if you don't) to every lot I saw. But if only a single bird came into view, I used to say 'good morning, sir, and good morning to your wife over the hedge' (although invisible) – the reason being that, according to the jingle about magpies,

One for sorrow
Two for mirth

No one courts sorrow, but mirth is a different thing. The jingle goes on:

Three for a wedding
Four for a birth
Five for silver
Six for gold
Seven for a secret
Never to be told
Eight for heaven
Nine for hell
Ten for the devil's very own sel'.

One old fellow told me this tale that happened when he was at school. It was at the annual school treat given by the Lord and Lady of the Manor. Her Ladyship was going along a long line of village lads asking each of them their names. She got to one boy called Hugh Halbitch. 'What's your name?' she enquired, in a highfalutin voice. The country lad, not sounding his h's, replied what sounded like, 'You old bitch, Ma'am.' The lady went scarlet. 'What did you say, you insolent child?' she cried. He repeated innocently, 'You old bitch, Ma'am.'

Needless to say there was an explanation called for from the boy's teacher!

During the walks and talks I collected quite a few more Cotswold words and sayings:

Yutting	eating
Empt	to empty
Mumchanchin'	thinking, day-dreaming
Crack yer jaw	to put your talk on
In the burra	to shelter out of the cold wind
Champin' yer grub	chewing your food
Blow yer bays out	to eat until you are full up
Gawpin'	to stare (what be gawpin' at)
Momblin'	mumbling or chattering
Famold	famished
Skellinton	skeleton
Sharlotts	shallots
Chimmock	chimney
Chibbles	onion shoots
Dockety	over-dressed woman ('ʼers all dockety')
Hawsens or *azzies*	haw berries
Egg pegs, hedge pigs or ag pags	sloe berries
Etchumin	sneezing
Slomocky	untidy
Issdy	yesterday
Plaze meself	please myself
A sheep's weskit (waistcoat)	a breast of lamb

Of a mean man 'twas said, 'He was that mean 'eed 'ett 'is mate [meat] raw tu save avin' tu cook it.'

Of a chattery woman 'twas said, ''Er gabbles like an old goose, dang me if er dunt.'

At a marriage service the vicar asked a country fellow, 'Will you take this woman to be your wedded wife?'
Groom: 'Thas what I brought 'er yer for wasent it?'

Mr Wooldridge, whose farm is adjacent to the village church, told me of an old Nympsfield custom that used to be carried out when people got married in the church:

After the wedding party had gone into church some of the young men of the village used to tie the churchyard gates together with strong rope, and so that it couldn't be untied easily they fixed bunches of stinging nettles all round the knots. Then when the bride and groom came out, the groom was forced to lift his bride over the gates. If the bride was a bit on the heavy side then they had to climb over the rather high churchyard wall.

'Do the lads of the village ever play that trick on newly-weds these days?' I asked Mr Wooldridge.

'Oh, yes, just occasionally,' he replied.

Index of Place Names